More glamorous

Beaded Jewelry

BRACELETS, NECKLACES, EARRINGS, AND RINGS

More glamorous Beaded Jewelry

BRACELETS, NECKLACES, EARRINGS, AND RINGS

CREATIVE HOMEOWNER
Home Arts

M. T. Ryan

CREATIVE HOMEOWNER®, Upper Saddle River, New Jersey

CRE**A**TIVE
HOMEOWNER®

A Division of Federal Marketing Corp.
Upper Saddle River, NJ

MORE GLAMOROUS BEADED JEWELRY

SENIOR EDITOR: Carol Endler Sterbenz
SENIOR GRAPHIC DESIGN COORDINATOR: Glee Barre
GRAPHIC DESIGNER: Maureen Mulligan
EDITORIAL ASSISTANT: Nora Grace
TECHNICAL WRITER: Genevieve A. Sterbenz
TECHNICAL EDITOR: Emily Harste
PHOTO RESEARCHER: Robyn Poplasky
INDEXER: Schroeder Indexing Services
PRINCIPAL PHOTOGRAPHY: Damian Sandone
INSTRUCTIONAL PHOTOGRAPHY: Steven Mays
PRODUCER OF PHOTOGRAPHY: Genevieve A. Sterbenz

CREATIVE HOMEOWNER

VP/PUBLISHER: Timothy O. Bakke
PRODUCTION DIRECTOR: Kimberly H. Vivas
ART DIRECTOR: David Geer
MANAGING EDITOR: Fran J. Donegan

Nymo® is a registered trademark of the Belding Heminway Company Corp.
Transite® is a registered trademark of the Roddy Recreation Products, Inc. Corp.
Delica® is a registered trademark of the Miyuki Shoji Co., Ltd.
Thread Heaven® is a registered trademark of Adam Beadworks
Fun-Tak® is a registered trademark of the National Starch and Chemical Corp.
Acculon® Tigertail is a registered trademark of the Cablestrand Corp.

Current Printing (last digit)
10 9 8 7 6 5 4 3 2

More Glamorous Beaded Jewelry, First Edition
Library of Congress Control Number: 2007938377
ISBN-10: 1-58011-408-3
ISBN-13: 978-1-58011-408-0
Manufactured in the United States of America

CREATIVE HOMEOWNER®
A Division of Federal Marketing Corp.
24 Park Way
Upper Saddle River, NJ 07458
www.creativehomeowner.com

Acknowledgments

Thanks go to: Carol E. Sterbenz, senior editor, whose inspiration and guidance made this book possible. Thanks also to photographers Damian Sandone and Steven Mays for capturing the essence of each piece of jewelry; to producer of photography, Genevieve A. Sterbenz, for a job well done; and to Maureen Mulligan, designer; Nora Grace, editorial assistant; and to technical editor Emily Harste for pulling all the elements together in one volume.

CONTENTS

INTRODUCTION

BRACELETS

12 Pastel Cloud
A frothy tangle of crocheted wire holds pearls in a sweet confection on this cuff bracelet with a pretty toggle clasp.

18 Liquid Gold
Highly polished gold nuggets are woven into precise rows to make a sophisticated wristband with a pearl closure.

22 Quarry
Tablets of patterned agate alternate with black hematite beads on this sleek 30s-style bracelet.

26 Starburst
Glittering crystal beads are scattered on spiky strands on this playful cuff bracelet made of memory wire.

NECKLACES

30 Willow Branch
Delicate branches are wrapped in fine gold wire and accented by berries and buds on this elegant necklace.

36 Floating Pearls
A scattering of luminous pearls in gemstone colors float on a trio of gold strands that twinkle with light.

40 Teardrop
A single, perfect crystal in honey-gold drops from a profusion of beads in rainbow colors on this flirty necklace.

44 Sunrise
A mix of beads in persimmon, peridot, and lavender sparkle on this 30s-style necklace.

50 Trio
Three round tablets with scribble patterns form a pendant on this hoop-style necklace.

54 Trefoil
A single briolette in a pale-honey color hangs from a delicate trio of aqua petals on this dainty necklace.

60 Venetian Swirl
Reminiscent of prized Murano glass, shapely beads are patterned with whorls of color on this elegant necklace.

64 Cascade
Quartz chunks and smooth glass beads in aubergine, rose, and amethyst are scattered on this illusion-style necklace.

PENDANTS

70 Spring Peas
Pendants in a rainbow of color dangle from graceful strands on this lariat-style necklace.

74 Ruby Drop
A large faceted ruby hangs from a sleek neoprene cord on this pendant-style necklace.

78 Starfish
A mix of pearls the color of moonlight encrusts a star-shaped pendant.

84 Infinity
A continuous loop of gleaming gold seed beads cradles an oversized pearl on this pendant.

90 Waterlily
Glowing gold disks with pearls cling to a segmented tendril on this elegant pendant.

96 Deco Harvest
A cluster of plump berries—reminiscent of the Art Deco era's Bakelite—dangles from a pretty chain.

102 Classic Acorns
Water-clear ovals are topped with graceful caps and accented with a velvet bow on this brooch and pendant.

EARRINGS AND RINGS

108 Caribbean Waters
Delicate teardrop-shaped briolettes swing below faceted bicones in bright aqua on these elegant drop earrings.

112 Zigzag
Lustrous silver-wrapped wire is bent into soft angles and threaded with pearls on these dangly earrings.

116 Les Anciennes
Light-catching cubic zirconia swing from pearl-studded pendulums on these sophisticated earrings.

120 Full Moon
A brushed silver disk forms a glowing halo around a simple moonstone on this contemporary-style ring.

126 Retro Modern
Polished silver disks and tubes combine with beads on these space-age earrings.

130 Bouquet
A cluster of dainty flowers rests on top of a ruby-red ring.

TOOLS

134 Beading Basics

MATERIALS

140 Beads
143 Strands
145 Findings

TECHNIQUES

148 Stringing Beads
152 Weaving Beads
158 Crimping Strand Material
160 Working with Wire

171 WORKING INDEX OF TECHNIQUES
172 RESOURCES
174 INDEX

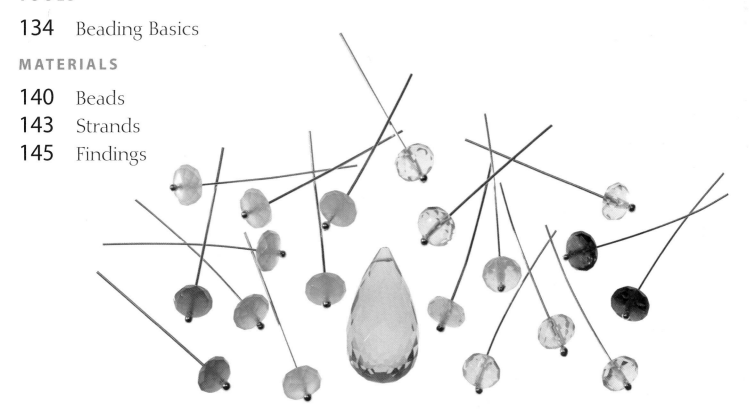

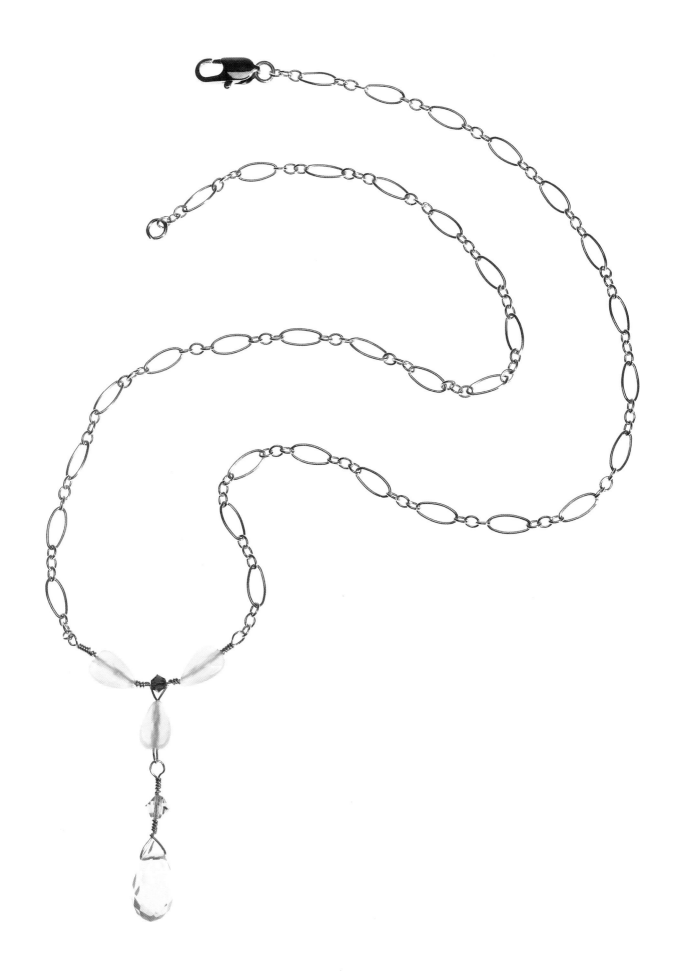

Introduction

MORE GLAMOROUS BEADED JEWELRY is a follow up to the earlier *Glamorous Beaded Jewelry*, which explored and demystified basic beading techniques to create elegant pieces of jewelry. *More Glamorous Beaded Jewelry* breaks new ground by using simple techniques in clever new ways to achieve glamorous and professional results. In this new volume, *More Glamorous Beaded Jewelry: Bracelets, Necklaces, Earrings, and Rings* present over 25 completely new and exciting projects that range from easily strung, but colorfully coordinated, bracelets, necklaces, and earrings to more complex and superbly elegant designs that feature bead weaving and wrapping and crocheting wire. Fresh trends in designing with lustrous beads and metallic finishes are also explored and augmented with ways to add subtle metal treatments that require no soldering or metalworking. Included in the work are clear step-by-step instructions that are accompanied by helpful diagrams and gorgeous color photography that captures every sparkling detail of the original designs. The comprehensive beading tutorial and source section are updated and enlarged, creating an inspiring and practical guide to making designs to suit your own unique style.

M Ryan

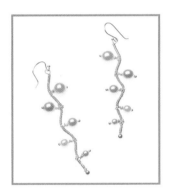   

The Collection

Completely new and exciting, "The Collection" features a dazzling array of bracelets, necklaces, rings, earrings, and pendants—each designed with imagination and careful attention to detail. Whether you are looking for an elegant pendant, a bracelet made from gold nuggets, or a necklace that glitters with crystals, More Glamorous Beaded Jewelry will show you how to make each signature piece.

lustrous pearls glow in
a nimbus of light

Pastel Cloud

Crocheted wire is an ideal base for supporting a large number of beads

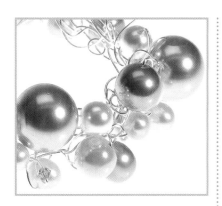

without drooping, while still keeping a light and airy look. Even the very large pearls on the "Pastel Cloud" bracelet stay in place because they are reasonably balanced along the length of the crocheted band. Varying sizes of pearls in a related palette unifies the composition. The silky luster of lavender, peach, copper, and green pearls is offset by the sparkle of the pink crystals—each discreetly woven into the pearl bracelet.

MATERIALS

- 3 round glass pearls, copper, 14mm dia.
- 7 round glass pearls in assort. colors, 9mm dia.:
     4 lavender
     3 green
- 4 freshwater pearls in assort. colors, 8mm dia. x 8mm thick:
     3 moss green
     1 copper
- 10 round glass pearls, white, 7mm dia.
- 12 freshwater pearls in assort. colors 5mm dia. x 6mm long:
     10 peach
     2 white
- 4 Austrian-crystal bicones, pink, 3mm dia.
- Wire, sterling-silver, 24-gauge
- 2 jump rings, sterling-silver, 5mm dia.
- Toggle clasp, sterling-silver, 12mm dia.

TOOLS

- Ruler
- Crochet hook (optional)
- Wire cutters
- Chain-nose pliers
- Round-nose pliers
- Bent-nose pliers
- Emery cloth, 400-grit

Making a Pastel Cloud Bracelet

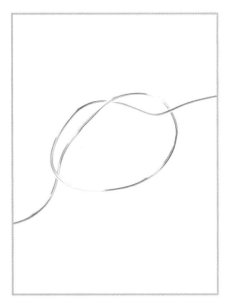 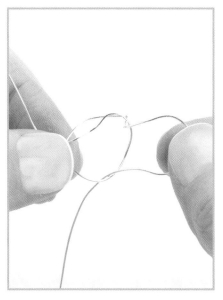 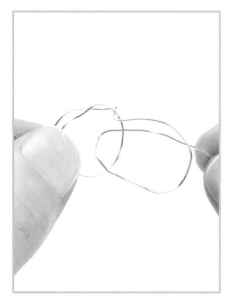

1 Pull approximately 18 in. (45.7cm) of wire from the spool. Do not cut it. For first loop, tie a loose square knot 2 in. (5.1cm) from the end. Note: when the knot is tied, have the short wire cross behind the knot and the long wire cross in front.

2 Hold the loop with one hand, and grasp the long wire with the other hand, 1 in. (2.5cm) from the knot. Bring the long wire behind the loop, and pull a loop through the center with one finger. Pull the loop off to the right.

3 Release the loop made in step 2. Grasp the long wire, and bring it up and behind this same loop. Note: this technique is adapted from crochet, but instead of yarn, wire is used to make the loops.

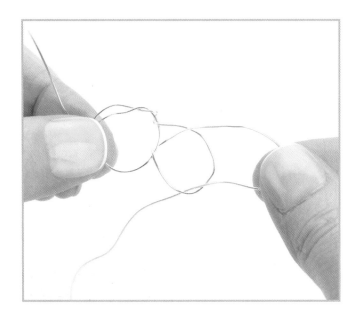 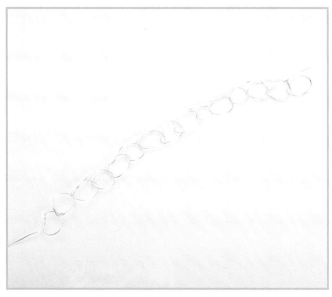

5 Pull the loop to the right.

6 Repeat steps 3–5 for 6 in. (15.2cm), or as desired. Use wire cutters to cut the crocheted band from the spool leaving a 2-in. (5.1cm) tail.

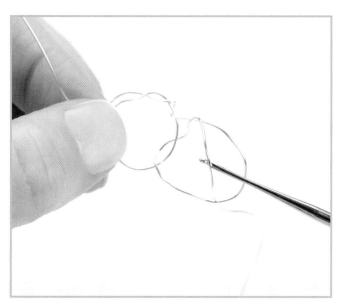

4 Pull a loop through the center using your finger or a crochet hook.

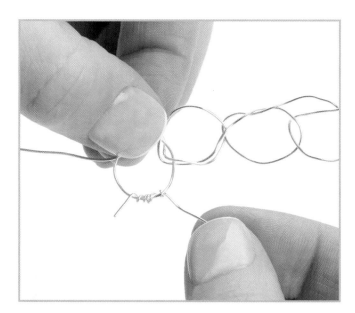

7 Use wire cutters to cut two 36-in. (91.4cm) lengths of wire. Set one length aside. Wrap one end of the wire around the first loop. Use hook-nose pliers to squeeze the cut end of the wire flush against the loop.

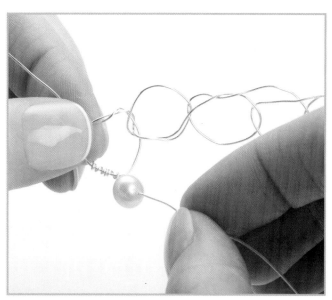

8 Thread the other end of the wire through one pearl.

Making a Pastel Cloud Bracelet

9 Loosely crochet the wire back and forth across the loops, adding pearls in different sizes and colors and working across to the end of the bracelet. Secure the end of the wire to the last loop as in step 7.

10 Wrap the end of the third length of wire around the first loop. Repeat steps 8–9, adding pearls and bicones to fill in any gaps.

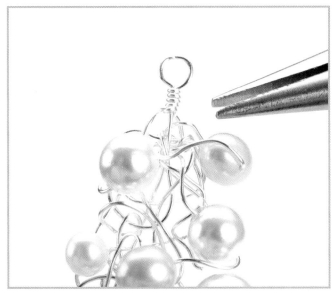

13 Grasp the loop with the chain-nose pliers. Use bent-nose pliers to continue wrapping the wire down the stem. Use wire cutters to trim away any excess wire. Use emery cloth to smooth the rough wire end.

14 Use chain-nose pliers to squeeze the cut end of the wire flush against the stem.

11 Make a wrapped-wire loop using the wire tail at one end of the bracelet. Use chain-nose pliers to grasp the wire ¼ in. (6mm) from the base Turn the pliers away from you to bend the wire at a 90-deg. angle.

12 Use round-nose pliers to grasp the wire ⅛ in. (3mm) from the bend. Rotate the pliers toward the bend. Wrap the wire around one jaw of the pliers, crossing the wire in front of the vertical stem to make a loop. Wrap the wire end around the stem.

15 Repeat steps 11–14 on the other end of the bracelet.

16 Use chain-nose and bent-nose pliers to open one jump ring. Thread one end of the jump ring through a wrapped-wire loop and the ring portion of the toggle clasp. Close the jump ring. Repeat this step at the other end, using the remaining jump ring and bar section of the toggle clasp.

glints of aqua
and lime color sparkle
in a stream of gold

Liquid Gold

A woven band of 24kt. gold-plated beads is accented

with single beads in gemstone colors and a lustrous pearl closure. The "Liquid Gold" bracelet uses extremely small Delica beads that are precisely cut, making them perfect for weaving the even-count flat peyote stitch that is used to create the sophisticated bracelet. The beads' precise shape allows them to "lock" together in perfect rows, producing a finished band that looks as fluid as molten gold.

MATERIALS

- *Delica seed beads , size 11/0, 2 4-gram tubes (approx. 800 beads each) 24kt. bright gold-plated: (Note: approx. 816 beads are needed.)*
    - *4 lime green*
    - *4 aqua blue*
- *1 round glass pearl, pink, 8mm dia. x 6mm long*
- *1 bobbin nonmetallic Nymo nylon thread, gold, size B*
- *Cyanoacrylate gel (instant glue)*

TOOLS

- *Ruler*
- *Scissors*
- *Beading needle, #10*
- *Chain-nose pliers*
- *Toothpick*

19

Making a Liquid Gold Bracelet

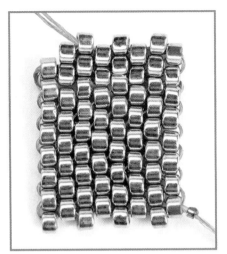

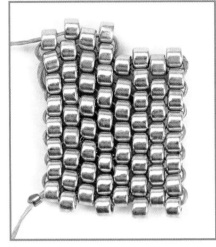

1 To begin, read "Weaving Beads" on pages 152 to 157. String a stopper bead onto a double strand of Nymo thread 24 in. (61.0cm) long. Row 1: string on eight gold beads. Rows 2–92: follow the bead layout right, adding the aqua and lime beads where indicated.

2 Row 93: for this first short row, stop beading after the fourth bead from the previous row. Note: do not continue across to finish the row. Row 94: string on a bead; pick up a bead from the previous row; add a bead; and pick up the last bead from the previous row. Turn the strip over.

6 Weave the needle through the beads of rows 112 and 92 so that the narrow strip forms a loop. Do not cut the thread. To reinforce the closure, weave the needle through the remaining beads on row 92. At the end of the row, weave the needle back through the beads to the center of the band where it splits. Insert the needle through the beads to the front, below the split. Bring the needle to the back. Cut off the needle. Working close to the beads, double knot the thread ends. Apply a drop of glue; let it dry; and trim the threads close to the knot. Use the needle to open the knot next to the stopper bead. Remove the stopper bead (from step 1). Tie the thread end into a square knot. Apply a drop of glue; let it dry; and trim off any excess thread.

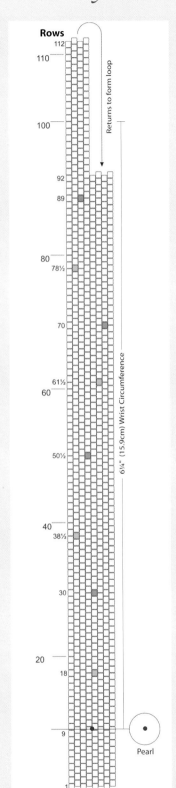

Rows

112
110
100
92
89
80
78½
70
61½
60
50½
40
38½
30
20
18
9
1

Returns to form loop

6¼" (15.9cm) Wrist Circumference

Pearl

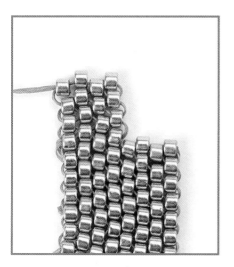

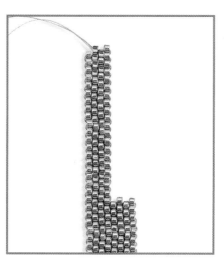

3 Rows 95–112: continue to bead the rows of four beads as in step 2.

4 After beading row 112, stop and position the band so that the narrow strip is on the left-hand side.

5 Bring the narrow strip around until it meets the edge of the band at row 92. Note: the two ends should match. If they don't, count the rows again, and add or subtract a row.

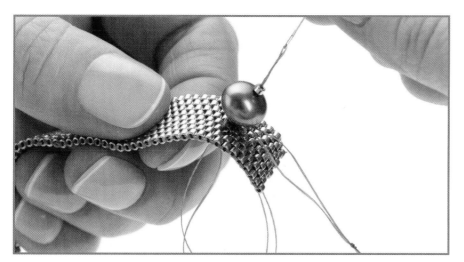

7 Test-fit the band to your wrist. Adjust the postion of the pearl if the band is too loose. Thread the needle with a 12-in. (30.5cm) length of thread. Don't knot the ends. Insert the needle from the front of the band to the back between beads 4 and 5 of row 9 (see the red dot on the bead layout). Leave a 1½-in. (3.8cm) tail of thread on the front. Bring the needle to the front through the center of row 10. String on the pearl and one gold seed bead. Have a ¼-in. (3mm) thread between the pearl and the band. Insert the needle back through the pearl to secure the seed bead. Bring the needle to the back at row 9, and return to the front at row 10.

8 Wrap the thread attached to the needle around the thread below the pearl 3–4 times. Cut off the needle. Working close to the beads, tie the ends together using a square knot. Apply a drop of glue; let it dry; and trim off any excess thread.

each perfectly polished stone
glows with layered color

Quarry

This easy-to-make bracelet is a study in contrasts—the high polish of agate, with its striped patterns and warm vibrant colors, complements the satin sheen of translucent jade in cool green. The dense silver-black tone of the hematite punctuates the stylistic theme.

The appeal of the "Quarry" bracelet is that no separate closure is needed, as an elastic line holds even heavy stones and allows the bracelet to be slipped on easily, fitting loosely on the wrist without slipping off.

MATERIALS

- 3 striped agate rectangles, orange, brown, and white, 20mm wide x 30mm long x 4mm thick
- 3 jade ovals, pale green, 20mm wide x 25mm long x 5mm thick
- 6 round hematite beads, 6mm dia.
- Elastic stringing cord, clear, 1mm dia.

TOOLS

- Ruler
- Scissors
- Paper clip
- Cyanoacrylate (instant glue), quick-set
- Toothpick

Making a Quarry Bracelet

1 Cut a 9-in. (22.9cm) length of elastic using scissors. Use a knot to secure one end of the elastic to a paper clip.

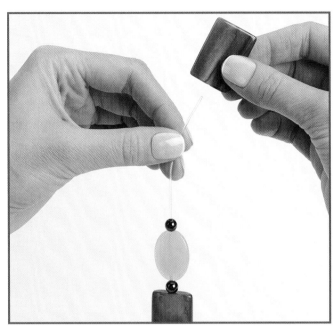

2 On the opposite end of the elastic, string on one agate bead, one hematite bead, one jade bead, and another hematite bead. Repeat this pattern twice.

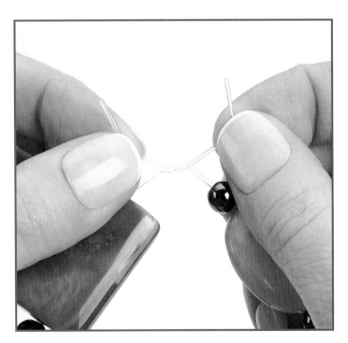

3 Hold both elastic ends close to the beads, and cut off the paper clip. Tie a square knot, pulling the elastic slightly to bring the beads closer together. Trim the elastic, leaving $3/16$-in. (5mm) tails.

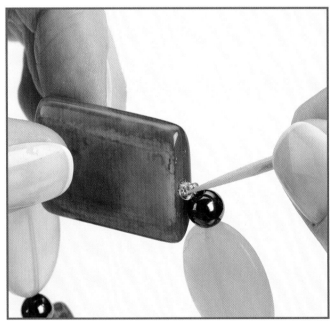

4 Apply a drop of glue to the knot; then pull the other end of the elastic to seat the knot inside the hole, using a toothpick, if necessary.

Agate comes in beautiful variegated colors. The "Quarry" bracelet features agate stones that are striped; when their markings run vertically, horizontally, or diagonally, they add interesting pattern to a design. Agates also come in contrasting textures—smooth, mottled, and splotchy.

variations

UNDERSTATED DRAMA

Simple shapes emphasize the striated and mottled textures of the stones used in these three bead patterns. When planning your design, consider mixing large stones in a quiet palette—tea, smoke, evergreen, slate, clay, and teak—with small round beads in honey, melon, persimmon, and cinnabar to add staccato notes of dramatic color.

a radiant constellation of
celestial crystals

Starburst

The "Starburst" bracelet combines bouncy coils of memory wire

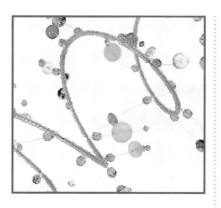

and transparent monofilament to create a piece of jewelry that is always on the move. The heavy stringing material supports decorative beads, which are glued in place, making knotting and crimping them unnecessary. What is especially appealing about the bracelet are the colors—crisp grassy green, soft sky blue, and blue-green shades that deepen the layered effect.

MATERIALS

- 5 faceted round beads, assort. opaque colors, 10mm dia.: 2 celadon, 3 pale blue
- 3 glass bicones, clear peridot, 8mm dia.
- 1 faceted rondelle, opaque jade, 8mm dia. x 5mm long
- 3 faceted rondelles, opaque sky blue, 8mm dia. x 4mm long
- 7 faceted glass rondelles, assort. clear colors, 7mm dia. x 4mm long
- 4 glass bicones, clear peridot, 6mm dia.
- 4 faceted round Czech.-crystal beads, metallic emerald green, 6mm dia.
- 4 faceted round glass beads, clear, 6mm dia.
- 6 glass discs, clear sky blue, 6mm dia. x 2mm thick
- 45 faceted round Austrian-crystal beads, peridot, 4mm dia.
- 4 faceted round Austrian-crystal beads, metallic peridot, 4mm dia.
- 2 faceted round beads, silver-lined, 4mm dia.: 3 citron, 4 dark green
- 16 Austrian-crystal bicones, assort. colors, 2mm dia.: 7 green, 7 sky blue, 2 olive green
- 8 round Austrian-crystal beads, assort. colors, 2mm dia.: 4 pale green, 4 sky blue
- 1 hank seed beads, frosted melon, size 12/0
- 2 half-drilled round memory-wire end beads, silver, 3mm dia.
- Other: memory wire, silver, bracelet weight; monofilament, clear, 5mm dia.; fast-set cyanoacrylate (instant glue)

TOOLS

- Memory-wire cutters
- Wire cutters
- Pliers: round-nose; chain-nose
- Tweezers

27

Making a Starburst Bracelet

1 Use memory-wire cutters to cut four and one-half loops of memory wire from the coil.

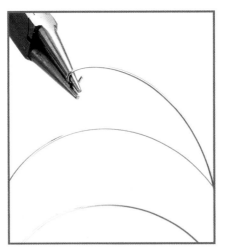

2 Use round-nose pliers to bend one end of the wire into a ⅛-in. (3mm) loop. Use chain-nose pliers to squeeze the loop against the wire. *Note:* the loop will prevent the beads from sliding off the wire. It will be cut off in step 10.

3 Thread the opposite end of the memory wire through the seed beads, sliding them along the wire to the loop. Leave 2 in. (5.1cm) of wire unbeaded. Repeat step 2, and make a loop in the end of the memory wire.

7 Repeat steps 4–6 to tie 44 more strands to the memory wire, spacing them ½ in. (13mm)–¾ in. (19mm) apart.

8 Place the bracelet on your work surface. Add one or two beads to each strand, working around the bracelet until all of the strands have beads in a pleasing array. Thread large beads on the strand first; use smaller beads as you move outward; and place the tiniest beads last.

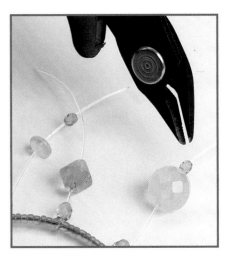

9 Secure each bead by sliding the bead aside, applying glue to the strand, and sliding the bead on top of the glue. Let the glue dry. Use wire cutters to trim the strand ends at varying lengths.

4 Cut 45 4-in. (10.2cm) strands of filament. Slide the beads to the loop end of the wire. Use a square knot to tie one strand to the wire, ½ in. (1.3cm) from the loop. Secure the knot with a drop of glue.

5 Thread both ends of the strand through a 4mm round peridot bead.

6 Secure the bead by separating the strands and adding a drop of glue between them. Let the glue dry. Use wire cutters to trim one strand flush with the top of the bead.

10 Use memory-wire cutters to cut off one loop in the wire. Apply glue to the end. Push the memory-wire end bead onto the end. Let the glue dry. Slide the beads to the finished end. Trim the other end of the wire to ¼ in. (6mm). Glue on the memory-wire end bead. Let the glue dry.

●●● design tip ●●●

The colorway of your bracelet can be easily translated into any palette you like. Take a look at a color wheel for ideas for new color combinations. Select a single unifying color, such as red, then add a secondary color that is situated next to or near the main color, such as red-orange or red-violet, to make a layered bracelet with a sophisticated tonal range.

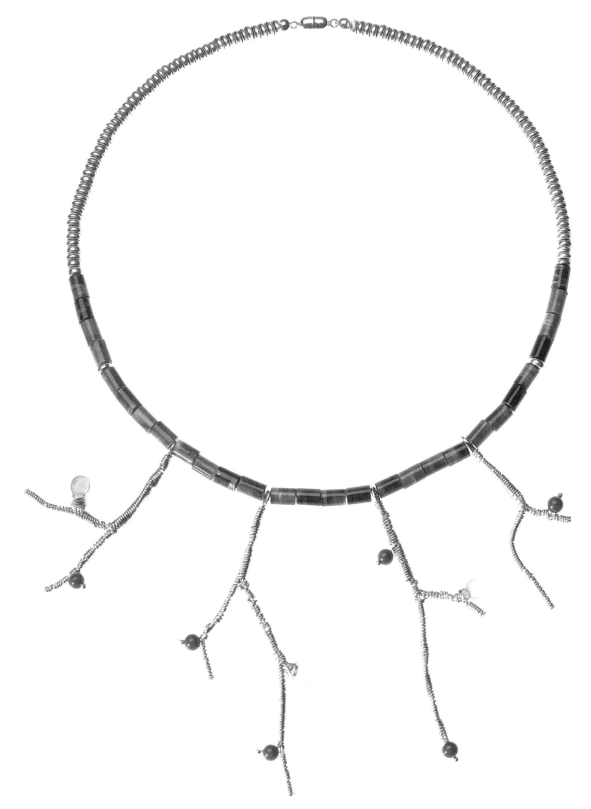

delicate new shoots
burst from young twigs

Willow Branch

With its natura-listic branches accented with berries and leaves, "Willow Branch" is a modern inter-pretation of spring. Its sculptural quality is achieved by wrapping thin gold wire around heavier core wire. To achieve a professional-looking wrap, make sure that the berry and leaf stems are flush against the core wire before entwining them with the thin wire. In this way, the interior struc-ture "disappears" neatly underneath the wire wraps.

MATERIALS

- *2 faceted jade briolettes, mint green, 5mm wide x 7mm long x 3mm thick*
- *1 faceted jade briolette, kelly green, 5mm wide x 7mm long x 3mm thick*
- *6 round garnets, red, 4mm dia.*
- *28 tiger's-eye tubes, 4mm dia. x 6mm long*
- *120 (approx.) discs, silver, 4mm dia. x 1mm thick. Note: a 7-in. length (17.8cm) is needed.*
- *6 headpins with 2mm ball ends, gold, 24-gauge, 1½ in. (38mm) long*
- *Wire, gold-plated with copper core, 20-gauge*
- *Wire, gold-plated, 26-gauge*
- *Scrap wire, silver, 24- to 28-gauge*
- *Transite*
- *2 crimp beads, silver, 3mm*
- *2 crimp-bead covers, silver, 4mm*
- *1 magnetic barrel clasp, silver*

TOOLS

- *Ruler*
- *Wire cutters*
- *Round-nose pliers*
- *Chain-nose pliers*
- *Crimping pliers*
- *Photocopier (to enlarge patterns)*

Making a Willow Branch Necklace

1 Use wire cutters to cut four lengths of 20-gauge wire: 4 in. (10.2cm); 5¼ in. (13.3cm); 4¼ in. (10.8cm); and 3½ in. (8.9m). Set three aside. Note: each of these wires is a core wire for one branch.

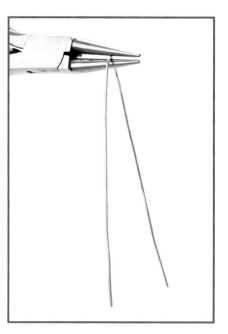

2 To create the hanging loop for branch **C,** use round-nose pliers to grasp the middle of the wire. Bend the wire in half.

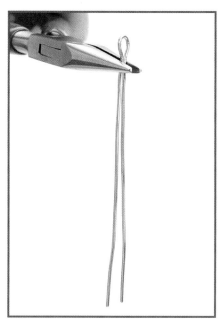

3 Use chain-nose pliers to squeeze the wires together at the base of the loop.

7 To add a red "berry" to branch **C,** thread one red garnet onto a headpin.

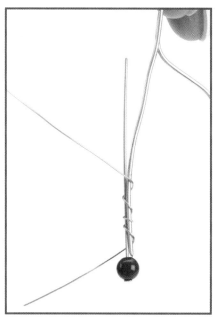

8 Place the beaded headpin, with the bead at the bottom, against the long segment of the branch. Use scrap wire to temporarily secure the headpin to the branch wire.

9 To add a berry at the top of the branch, thread one red garnet onto a headpin. Use chain-nose pliers to grasp the headpin above the bead, and turn the pliers to bend a 90-deg. angle.

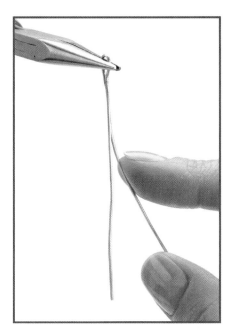

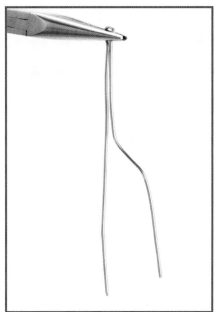

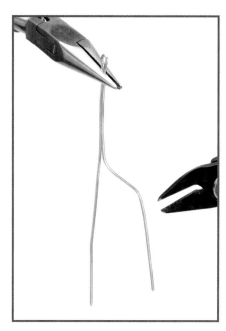

4 Enlarge the branch patterns 140 percent. Place the wire from step 3 onto the branch **C** pattern. Bend the right wire so that it matches the pattern line.

5 Continue to bend the wires as indicated in the pattern. Note: there will be one long segment and one slightly shorter segment; loop faces forward.

6 When branch **C** is shaped, use wire cutters to trim away any excess wire making sure that the wire on the right matches the pattern.

10 With the bead toward the front of the branch, place the beaded headpin against the branch's long segment. Use scrap wire to temporarily secure the headpin to the branch wire.

branch patterns

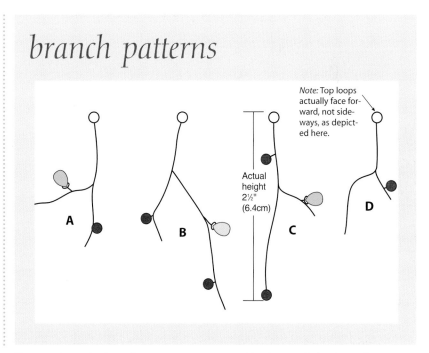

Note: Top loops actually face forward, not sideways, as depicted here.

Actual height 2½" (6.4cm)

A   B   C   D

Note: enlarge the branch patterns 140 percent. Use them to help shape the branches and to guide the placement of the leaves and berries.

11 For a leaf, cut a 6-in. (15.2cm) length of 26-gauge wire. Following the instructions on pages 166 to 167, make a wrapped loop with a stem using a mint-green briolette.

12 Place the leaf and stem against the short segment of the branch. Use scrap wire to temporarily secure the stem wire to the branch wire. Note: if you have never wrapped wire before, read "Wrapping Wire" on pages 162 to 163 before going to step 13.

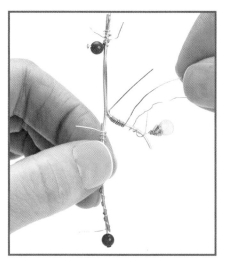

13 For wrapping wire, pull 4 in. (10.2cm) of 26-gauge wire from the spool. Hold branch **C** with one hand, and undo a few winds of scrap wire with the other hand. Hold a 1-in. (2.5cm) tail of wrapping wire against the main branch, and begin wrapping at the base of the short segment. Note: always wrap the short segments first, beginning at the base; then wrap the long segments.

16 Use wire cutters to cut a 20-in. (50.8cm) length of Transite. Secure one end of the Transite to the barrel clasp using a crimp bead and crimping pliers.

17 Use chain-nose pliers to cover the crimp bead with a crimp-bead cover.

18 String a 3⅛-in. (7.9cm) length of silver discs onto the Transite. Tuck the cut end of Transite into the discs.

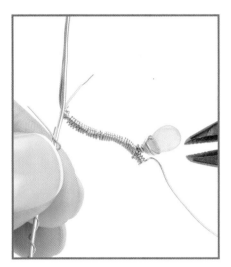

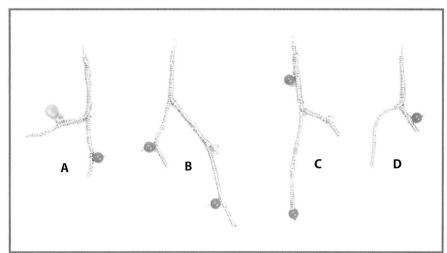

14 Wrap the wire toward the leaf, covering the leaf stem as you wrap. Undo a few winds of scrap wire before the entire segment is wrapped. When the leaf stem is secure, remove the remaining scrap wire. Trim the wrapping wire close to the segment. Use chain-nose pliers to squeeze the cut end of wire flush against the segment.

15 Use the techniques in steps 13–14 to secure the berries and to cover the main branch with wrapping wire. Begin just under the top loop. Continue down the branch, removing the scrap wire as you wrap. Follow steps 1–15 to make branches **A, B,** and **D.** Follow the patterns on page 33 to shape and trim each branch and to position the leaves and berries.

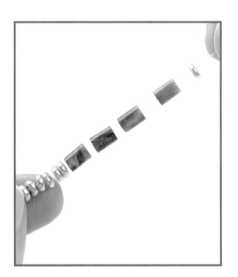

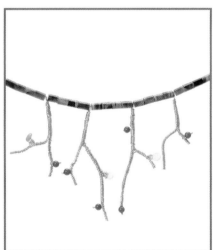

19 String on four tiger's-eye tubes, one silver disc, and four tiger's-eye tubes.

20 String on branches **A, B, C,** and **D,** each followed by four tiger's-eye tubes. End by stringing on one silver disc, four tiger's-eye tubes, and 3¹⁄₈ in. (7.9cm) of silver discs.

21 Secure the other end of Transite to the barrel clasp using a crimp bead and crimping pliers. Note: see step 18 for covering a crimp bead. Tuck the cut end of the Transite into the last beads; trim away any excess.

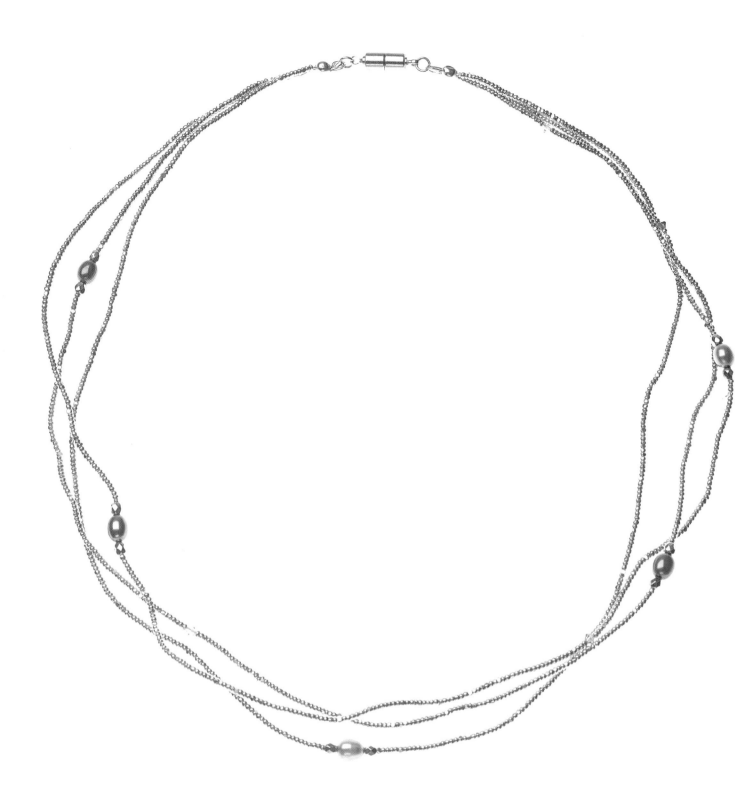

pearls in jewel tones "float" in a
delicate tangle of gold nuggets

Floating Pearls

Tiny matte-gold seed beads are highlighted by pearls and faceted glass beads that sparkle like little mirrors. The secret of the bouncing and floating strands of the "Floating Pearls" necklace is the wire that is the core of each strand. Thin, but strong and malleable, once it is beaded the wire retains its shape when bent. For a choker that rides close to the neck, make crinkly arches in the wire to shorten each strand. Or for a looser necklace, straighten the beaded wires.

MATERIALS

- 5 freshwater pearls, assort. colors, 5mm dia. x 6.5mm long:
  - 1 red
  - 1 green
  - 1 blue
  - 1 taupe
  - 1 copper
- 10 faceted round Czech-glass beads, gold, 3mm dia.
- 4 Austrian-crystal bicones, assort. colors, 3mm dia.:
  - 1 green
  - 1 blue
  - 1 fuchsia
  - 1 pink
- 1 hank of irregularly faceted seed beads, gold-plated, size 11. Note: 60" (1.5m) are needed.
- Wire, gold-plated with copper core, 26-gauge
- 2 crimp beads, gold, 3mm dia.
- 2 crimp-bead covers, gold, 4mm
- 2 jump rings, gold, 4mm dia.
- 1 magnetic barrel clasp, gold-plated, 5mm dia. x 10mm long

TOOLS

- Ruler
- Masking tape (optional)
- Wire cutters
- Round-nose pliers
- Crimping pliers
- Chain-nose pliers
- Tweezers
- Bent-nose pliers

••• Making a Floating Pearls Necklace

1 Use wire cutters to cut three 24-in. (61.0cm) lengths of wire, one for each strand. Set two aside. Note: the final length of each strand is approximately 18 in. (45.7cm); the extra length provides room to work with the wire.

2 Fold over one end of the wire ¾ in. (1.9cm) to prevent the beads from falling off. Straighten the other wire end. While holding the thread of seed beads, feed the wire's straight end through the bead holes, sliding the beads onto the wire for Strand A.

6 Use chain-nose pliers to bend the wire ends parallel with the beaded wires. Slide the crimp bead toward the loop and over the wire ends. Position the crimp bead just under the loop. Use crimping pliers to secure the crimp bead.

7 Use chain-nose pliers to conceal the crimp bead with a crimp-bead cover. Hold the wires at the other end of the strand. Slide the beads toward the finished ends, tucking each wire end into its strand of beads and using tweezers if necessary. Use wire cutters to trim off the folded wire. Repeat steps 4–7 at the other end, but make a loop close to the beads.

8 Working with the closed barrel clasp, thread an open jump ring through one loop of the necklace and a loop on one half of the barrel clasp. Use chain-nose and bent-nose pliers to close the jump ring. Repeat at the other end of the necklace to attach the second half of the barrel clasp.

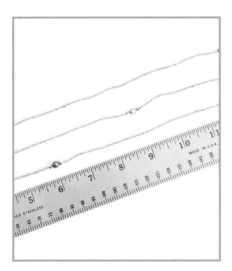

3 Use a ruler to check the measurement of the segment. Follow the beading diagram for strand A, and add the pearls, faceted gold beads, and bicones. Follow steps 2–3 to bead strands B and C.

4 Holding the ends even, gather the straight ends of wires A, B, and C together. Thread on a crimp bead, and slide it toward the seed beads.

5 Use round-nose pliers to grasp the wires ½ in. (1.3cm) from their ends. Rotate the pliers to form a loop.

beading layout

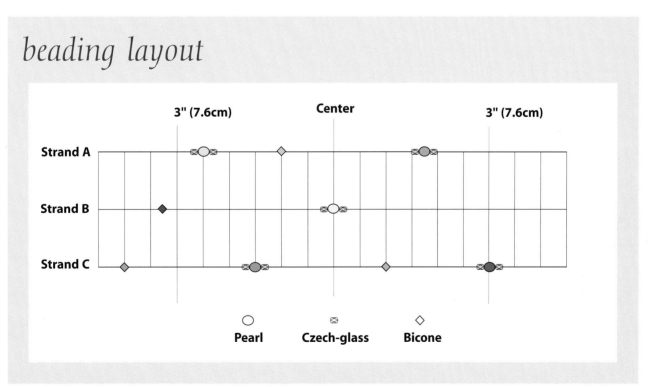

Note: the horizontal lines represent the beaded strands and indicate the position of the accent beads. The vertical lines indicate the approximate measurements of each beaded segment. Scale: one segment = 1 in. (The beads are not drawn to scale.)

like a thick drop of honey, a
gracefully from a rainbow of

Teardrop

The easy and shimmering movement of a faceted teardrop

and clusters of crystal rondelles makes this necklace fun to wear. In a shifting rainbow of color that moves from lavender, rich purple, persimmon, and honey gold to pale lime, peridot, teal, and aqua, sparkling crystal beads cascade from a gold chain hung with a single faceted teardrop that glows in the warmest shade of honey gold.

faceted teardrop falls sparkling crystals

MATERIALS

■ 1 faceted teardrop-shape crystal, amber, 15mm dia. x 30mm long

■ 30 faceted crystal rondelles in assorted colors, water clear, 6–8mm dia. x 3–6mm thick:
   2 lavender
   1 aubergine
   1 mauve
   1 fuchsia
   1 pink
   1 brown
   1 persimmon
   1 tan
   2 amber
   2 honey gold
   1 yellow
   2 beige
   2 pale lemon
   2 pale lime
   2 grass green
   3 peridot green
   2 olive green
   1 pale teal
   1 pale sky blue
   1 aqua blue

■ Wire, gold-plated with copper core, 26-gauge

■ 30 headpins with 2mm ball end, gold, 24-gauge, 1¼" (32mm) long

■ 18" (45.7cm) cable-link chain, gold, each link 2mm wide x 3mm long

■ 3 jump rings, gold, 4mm dia.

■ 1 lobster clasp, gold, 7mm wide x 12mm long

TOOLS

■ Ruler

■ Wire cutters

■ Chain-nose pliers

■ Bent-nose pliers

■ Round-nose pliers

Making a Teardrop Necklace

1 Use wire cutters to cut an 18-in. (45.7cm) length of chain.

2 See "Making a Wrapped Loop" on pages 166 to 167. Then make a wrapped loop on the amber crystal.

3 Use chain-nose and bent-nose pliers to open a jump ring. Thread the jump ring through the loop on the amber crystal and the center link of the chain. Close the jump ring.

7 Use your fingers to wrap the head-pin around one jaw of the pliers, and cross the wire stem in front to make a loop.

8 Insert the end of the headpin into the first link to the right of the crystal on the chain.

9 Grasp the loop with chain-nose pliers. Use your fingers or bent-nose pliers to wrap the headpin end around the stem. Continue wrapping from the loop down to the rondelle. Use wire cutters to cut away any excess wire. Use chain-nose pliers to squeeze the cut end flush against the stem.

4 Arrange the rondelles in a row on a flat surface, using the materials list as a guide; begin at the left with lavender and end at the right with aqua blue. Then thread the pale-lemon rondelle on a headpin.

5 Use chain-nose pliers to grasp the headpin ¼ in. (6mm) above the rondelle. To begin the wrapped loop, turn the pliers on a 90-deg. angle to bend the headpin.

6 Use round-nose pliers to grasp the headpin ⅛ in. (3mm) from the bend. Rotate the pliers toward the bend.

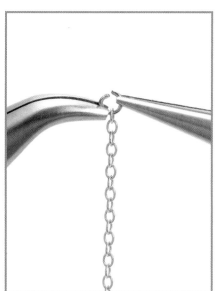

10 Repeat steps 4–9, adding the rondelles to the chain, following the color sequence shown above. Attach each rondelle to the next link in the chain.

11 Use chain-nose and bent-nose pliers to open a jump ring. Thread the jump ring through the last link at one end of the chain. Close the jump ring.

12 Thread an open jump ring through the lobster clasp and the last link at other end of the chain. Close the jump ring.

pendants in sublime colors
break like rays of a morning sun

Sunrise

The rich autumnal palette of the "Sunrise" necklace is built around the

warm persimmon glow of natural carnelian nuggets. The softer tones of lavender, peridot green, and topaz highlight the elegant glossy polish of the carnelians. Although the necklace appears complex, it is a straightforward stringing project. The wrapped loops on the pendant briolettes are strung along with the other beads, creating a crown of sparkling color.

MATERIALS

- 12 faceted carnelian, pillow shaped, persimmon, 12mm wide x 13–15mm long x 6mm thick
- 14 faceted carnelian nuggets, persimmon, 10mm wide x 11–14mm long x 5mm thick
- 6 faceted crystal briolettes, peridot, 9mm wide x 14mm long x 5mm thick
- 7 faceted crystal briolettes, yellow topaz, 9mm wide x 9mm long x 3mm thick
- 40 faceted round Austrian-crystal beads, lavender, 4mm dia.
- 13 oval beads, brushed gold, 4mm dia. x 8mm long
- Wire, gold, 26-gauge
- 2 crimp beads, gold, size 2
- 2 crimp-bead covers, gold, 3mm dia.
- 1 oval magnetic clasp, gold, 6mm dia. x 13mm long (19mm long with end rings)
- Transite

TOOLS

- Ruler
- Wire cutters
- Bent-nose pliers
- Chain-nose pliers
- Crimping pliers
- Tweezers

••• Making a Sunrise Necklace

1 Use wire cutters to cut 13 7-in. lengths (17.8cm) of wire. Set twelve wires aside.

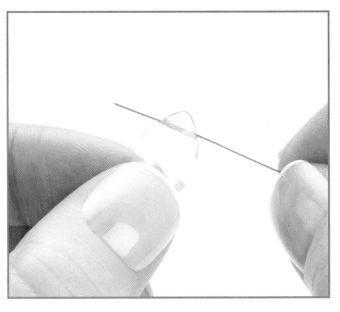

2 Thread one peridot briolette on the center of the wire.

5 Thread a gold oval bead onto the stem of the briolette.

6 Follow the directions on page 166 to make a wrapped loop to complete the briolette assembly. Set it aside. Repeat steps 2–6 for the remaining peridot and yellow-topaz briolettes.

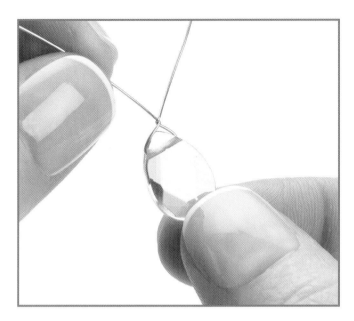

3 Bring the wires up, cross them, and twist them together once.

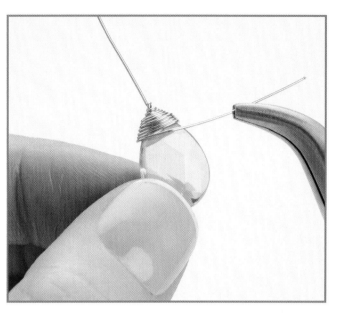

4 Hold one wire while using bent-nose pliers to wrap the other wire down around the top of the briolette. Trim off the excess wire. Use chain-nose pliers to press the wire end flush against the briolette.

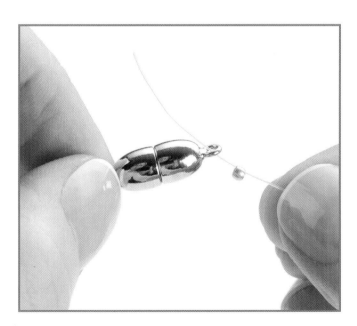

7 Use wire cutters to cut a 30-in. (76.2cm) length of Transite. Thread on a crimp bead. Thread the Transite through one end of the clasp.

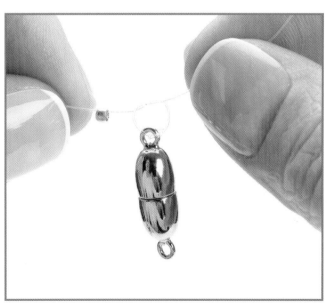

8 Tie a square knot in the Transite ½ in. (1.3cm) from the end, close to the clasp.

Making a Sunrise Necklace

9 Slide the crimp bead toward the clasp, over the end of Transite tail. Position the crimp bead just under the knot. Use crimping pliers to secure the crimp bead.

10 Use chain-nose pliers to conceal the crimp bead with a crimp cover.

variation

COOL COLORWAY

In the original "Sunrise" necklace, the beads are in a rich and warm autumnal palette. For a necklace in a cool colorway, combine beads in icy blue and pale green (right). Replace the pillow-cut carnelians with oval-shaped faceted quartz crystals in pale blue, and oval beads in brushed gold with those in gleaming silver.

11 String on one lavender bead and one small carnelian nugget. Tuck the end into the beads. Repeat the pattern six more times. String on one lavender bead, one yellow-topaz briolette assembly, one lavender bead, and one large carnelian nugget. Repeat the pattern 12 more times alternating between the peridot and yellow briolettes. End the last pattern repeat with one small carnelian nugget. String on one lavender bead and one small carnelian nugget. Repeat the pattern five more times and end with a lavender bead.

12 Thread on a crimp bead. Thread the end through the other end of the clasp. Repeat steps 8–9, making a knot close to the beads. Use tweezers to insert the end into the crimp bead. Use wire cutters to trim the end to ½ in. (1.3cm). Use tweezers to tuck the end into the beads.

●●●helpful tip●●●

The length of the "Sunrise" necklace is easily customized. The briolette pendants are centered on the strand with large carnelians; the small carnelians are used toward the clasp. Add or subtract small carnelians to adjust the length.

13 Use chain-nose pliers to conceal the crimp bead with a crimp-bead cover.

graduated round disks **and silver**
ovals fall **from a simple hoop**

Trio

The minimal, yet dramatic, geometry of "Trio" is achieved with just three

stones. Polished into perfectly round disks, their pale translucence is offset by the brushed-silver beads that separate them. The silver oval beads are chosen not only for their sensual shape, but for practical reasons—their tapered ends have small holes that fit neatly into the larger holes in the disks, keeping the beads aligned on the wire. The geometry of "Trio" can be accentuated by using disks in deeper tones, such as onyx.

MATERIALS

- 1 clear stone disk with beige veining, 30mm dia. x 6mm thick
- 1 clear stone disk with beige veining, 20mm dia. x 6mm thick
- 1 clear stone disk with beige veining, 13mm dia. x 6mm thick
- 1 oval bead, brushed silver, 5mm dia. x 12mm long
- 1 oval bead, brushed silver, 4mm dia. x 8mm long
- 1 oval bead, brushed silver, 3mm dia. x 5mm long
- 1 crimp-bead cover, silver, 3mm dia.
- 4" (10.2cm) wire, silver, 20-gauge
- 1 bead-and-loop pendant bail, silver; bead, 4mm dia.; loop, 3mm dia.
- 1 neck wire with ball-and-tube ends, silver, 16" (40.6cm) circumference (Note: one ball-tip is permanently attached.)

TOOLS

- Ruler
- Wire cutters
- Round-nose pliers
- Bent-nose pliers
- Chain-nose pliers
- Cyanoacrylate gel (instant glue)

Making a Trio Necklace

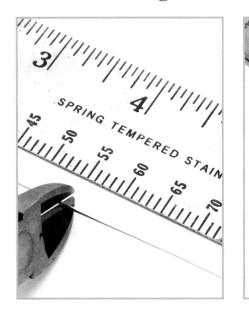

1 Use wire cutters to cut a 4-in. (10.2cm) length of wire.

2 Use round-nose pliers to make a loop at one end of the wire. Do not close the loop. See "Making a Wire Loop" on page 164 for more details.

3 Thread the largest oval bead and the largest disk onto the wire. Repeat twice more, moving from the largest disks and beads to the smallest.

7 Remove the ball-and-tubes from the end of the neck wire. Thread the bead of the pendant bail onto the neck wire.

Pendant Bails

When originating your own pendant designs, remember that the bail that holds the pendant to the necklace is a subtle, but important, design element that should be consistent in style and finish with the other components in your necklace design.

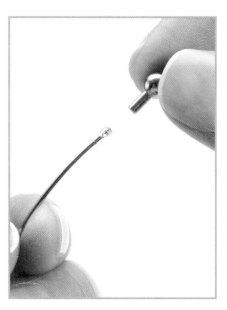

8 Apply a drop of glue to one end of the neck wire. Adhere the ball-and-tube to the end. Let the glue dry.

4 Use round-nose pliers to make a small loop below the smallest disk.

5 Use bent-nose pliers to conceal the loop with a crimp-bead cover.

6 Use bent-nose pliers to thread the open loop onto the loop of the pendant bail. Use chain-nose pliers to close the loop.

variation
SUBTLE CHANGES

The modern style of the elegant "Trio" necklace is signaled by simple geometry and a minimum number of design elements—round beads in graduated sizes and oval beads in brushed silver. For a subtle style change, substitute square beads (for the round) and oval beads with a bright finish (for the oval beads in a brushed finish).

a pendant in warm honey
extends from aqua-blue petals

Trefoil

A large hanging stone or bead is frequently the focal point of a necklace, but for a novel change, shift the focus of attention to the hanging point. In the "Trefoil" necklace, three pale aqua beads form "petals" around a center fuchsia crystal, creating a dainty arrangement that resembles a spring flower. Two petals are connected by their loops to gold links in the chain, continuing the delicate harmony of elements that characterizes the "Trefoil" design.

MATERIALS

- 1 faceted crystal briolette, teardrop shape, pale honey, 7mm dia. x 13mm long, head-drilled
- 3 faceted dyed-quartz briolettes, aqua, 5mm wide x 8mm long x 3mm thick, center-drilled
- 1 Austrian-crystal bicone, light olivine, 4mm
- 1 Austrian-crystal bicone, fuchsia, 3mm
- Wire, gold, 26-gauge
- 18" (45.7cm) figaro chain, gold, 3.5mm wide x 7mm long, oval links separated by small round links
- 2 jump rings, gold, 4mm dia.
- 1 lobster clasp, gold, ½ in. (13mm) long

TOOLS

- Ruler
- Wire cutters
- Chain-nose pliers
- Bent-nose pliers

Making a Trefoil Necklace

1 Use wire cutters to cut one 2-in. (5.1cm), one 3-in. (7.6cm), and one 6-in. (15.2cm) length of wire. Set them aside. Cut two 8½-in. (21.6cm) lengths of chain. Note: make each cut at a long oval link. Have three small links at both ends of each chain.

2 Thread the honey teardrop briolette onto 2 in. (5.1cm) of wire, ½ in. (1.3cm) from the end. Bend up the wires, and cross them.

5 Bend the 3-in.-long (7.6cm) wire in half. Thread the wrapped loop from the assembly in step 4 to the center of the wire.

6 Hold the wire ends together, and thread both of them through one aqua briolette. Slide the briolette to the wrapped loop. Separate the wire ends into a "V." Set the assembly aside.

3 Wrap the short wire three to four times around the long wire. Trim away any excess wire, and use chain-nose pliers to press the wire end flush against the long wire stem. Thread on the olivine bicone.

4 Follow the directions on pages 164 to 165, and make a wire loop above the bicone. Set the assembly aside.

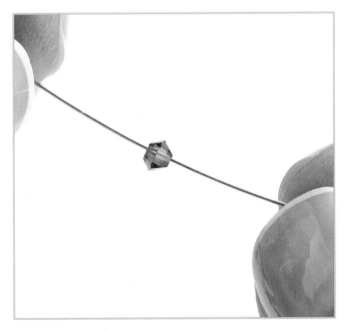

Working Tip

It is important that the wires that extend from the aqua briolette at the center bottom of the assembly are straight. Gently stroke them with your thumb and fingers to smooth them and to ensure that there are no kinks or bends in the wires.

7 Thread the fuchsia bicone on the 6-in.-long (15.2cm) wire, and center it on the wire. Position the assembly, horizontally, on your work surface.

Making a Trefoil Necklace

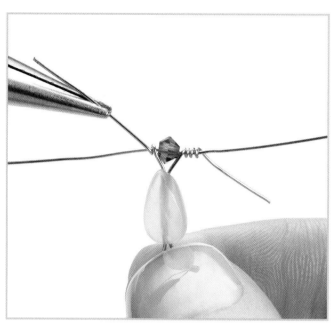

8 Position the assembly from step 6 on top of the 6-in.-long (15.2cm) wire and directly under the fuchsia bicone.

9 Use chain-nose pliers to wrap one end of the wire "V" five times around the 6-in.-long (15.2cm) wire at the right of the fuchsia bicone. Trim away any excess wrap wire. Use chain-nose pliers to press the end of the cut wire flush against the 6-in.-long (15.2cm) wire. Repeat for the other end of the wire "V."

11 Thread the same wire from step 10 through a loop at one end of a length of chain. Secure them together following the directions on page 165 for making a wrapped loop.

12 Repeat steps 10–11 to add the last aqua briolette, and secure it to the second length of chain on the other side.

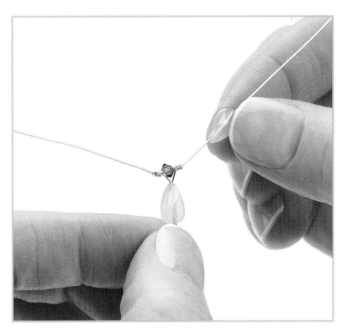

10 Thread one aqua briolette on 6-in.-long (15.2cm) wire to the right of the fuchsia bicone.

●●● **design tip** ●●●

Fine-gauge wire is used in the "Trefoil" necklace because it is thin enough to allow two lengths to pass through the aqua briolette that is positioned at the bottom center, while keeping the delicate sensibility of the design.

13 Use chain-nose and bent-nose pliers to attach a jump ring at one end of the chain.

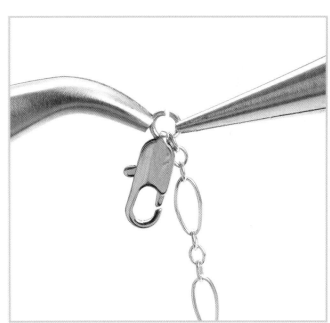

14 Use chain-nose and bent-nose pliers to thread one open jump ring through the other end of the chain and the lobster clasp. Close the jump ring.

colorful patterns swirl
around blown-glass beads

Venetian Swirl

The snow-white whorls and colorful patterns of these glamorous

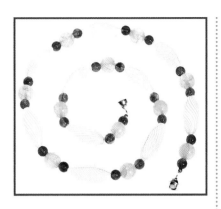

Venetian-style glass beads contrast softly with the rose and amethyst quartz beads that separate them. The beads are strung with Transite because it is strong enough to support the weight of the beads, and it is transparent so that it can barely be seen through the patterned glass. Taken together, the contrasting shapes and colorways of the beads create a necklace with sensuality and elegance.

MATERIALS

- *10 clear Venetian-style blown-glass oval beads with white stripes, 13mm dia. x 25mm long*
- *11 round quartz beads, rose, 10mm dia.*
- *22 round dyed-quartz beads, amethyst, 6mm dia.*
- *2 crimp beads, silver, 2mm dia.*
- *2 crimp-bead covers, silver, 3mm dia.*
- *1 oval magnetic clasp, silver, 8mm dia. x 12mm long*
- *Transite*

TOOLS

- *Ruler*
- *Wire cutters*
- *Crimping pliers*
- *Chain-nose pliers*
- *Toothpick*

Making a Venetian Swirl Necklace

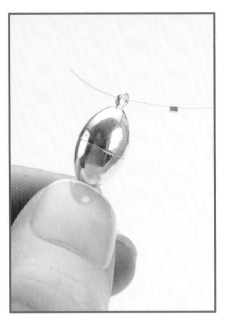

1 Use wire cutters to cut a 30-in. (76.2cm) length of Transite.

2 Thread a crimp bead onto one end of the Transite. Thread the Transite though the loop in the magnetic clasp.

3 Tie a square knot in the Transite, leaving a 1-in. (2.5cm) tail. Note: be careful not to trap the crimp bead in the knot.

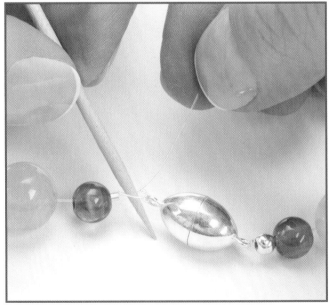

6 Thread on one amethyst bead, one rose bead, one amethyst bead, and one clear oval bead with stripes. Hide the Transite tail inside the beads. Repeat the beading pattern nine more times. Then thread on one amethyst bead, one rose bead, and one amethyst bead.

7 Repeat steps 2–4 at the other end of the Transite. Tie a knot, but before tightening it, use a toothpick to slide the knot close to the clasp. Leave room for the crimp bead and the crimp-bead cover between the clasp and the first bead. Note: trim the tail of Transite to 1 in. (2.5cm) when repeating step 3.

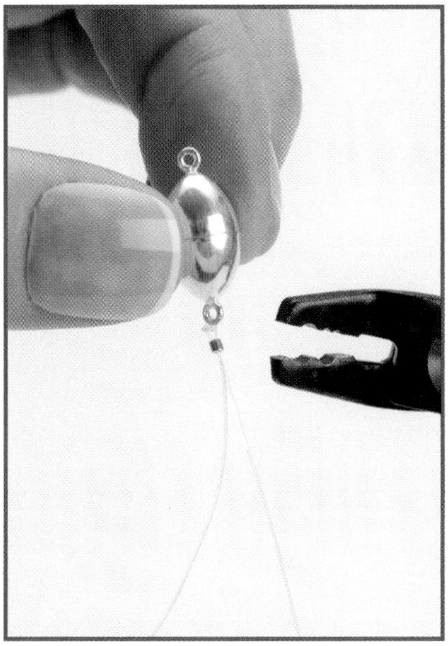

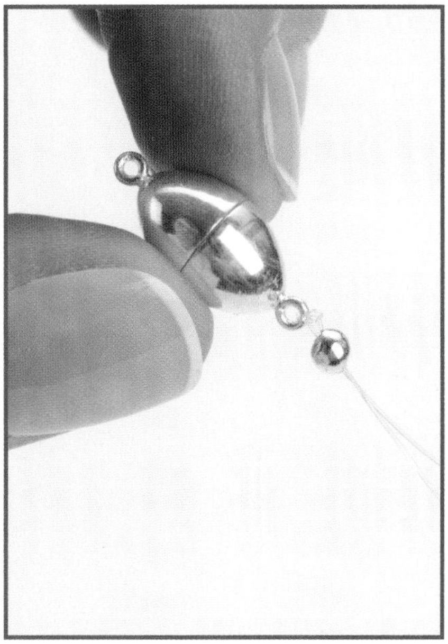

The Clasp

Although the hollow Venetian-style beads are lightweight, the quartz beads that separate them add weight to the necklace. Use a large clasp with a strong magnet to ensure that the necklace remains closed while it is worn.

4 Slide the crimp bead toward the knot and over the tail of Transite. Use crimping pliers to secure the crimp bead.

5 Use chain-nose pliers to conceal the crimp bead with a crimp-bead cover.

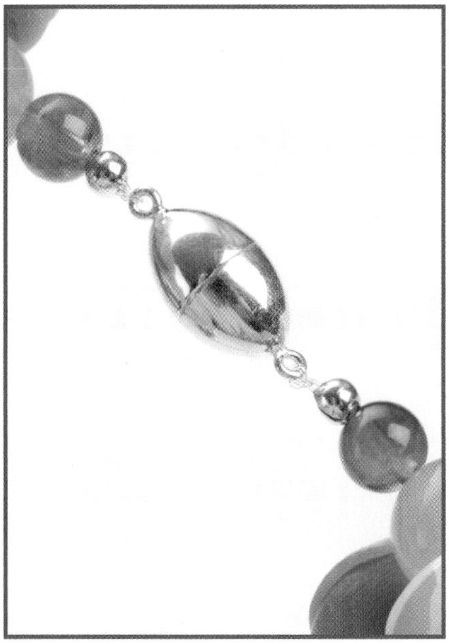

8 Use chain-nose pliers to cover the crimp bead with a crimp-bead cover. Hide the tail of Transite inside the beads.

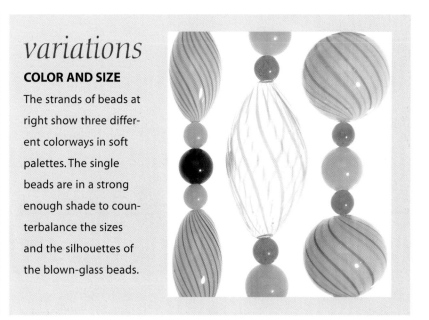

variations

COLOR AND SIZE

The strands of beads at right show three different colorways in soft palettes. The single beads are in a strong enough shade to counterbalance the sizes and the silhouettes of the blown-glass beads.

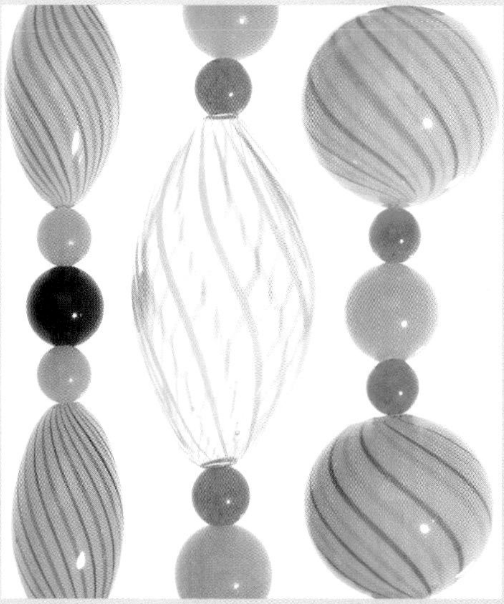

chunky crystals with sharp
angles radiate brilliant color

Cascade

The long strands of the "Cascade" necklace are worn swingy and low, allowing them to entwine for a pretty effect when the necklace is worn. The beads range in color from aubergine, plum, and wine to red and lavender. This narrow tonal range is accented by beads in lighter shades of pink, rose, and white that brighten the overall effect. The colors of the beads and the findings are closely related to the mauve of the strand material, creating a design with balance and harmony.

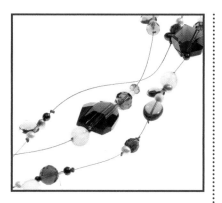

MATERIALS

- 5 faceted dyed-quartz nuggets, aubergine, (c), 22mm wide x 27mm long x 15mm thick
- 7 faceted clear briolettes, smoky quartz, (h), 10mm wide x 12mm long x 6mm thick
- 3 faceted clear dyed-quartz briolettes, dusty rose, (h), 10mm wide x 12mm long x 6mm thick
- 5 faceted opaque quartz briolettes, pink, (c), 10mm wide x 12mm long x 6mm thick
- 3 faceted clear round crystal beads, root beer, (c), 10mm dia.
- 3 faceted clear round crystal beads, amethyst, (c), 10mm dia.
- 3 faceted clear round crystal beads, amethyst, (c), 8mm dia.
- 4 round quartz beads, rose, 10mm dia.
- 3 clear ovals, coffee, (h), 11mm wide x 16mm long x 5mm thick
- 6 clear daggers, hot pink, 6mm wide x 16mm long x 3mm thick
- 3 faceted clear rondelles, dark pink, (c), 8mm dia. x 6mm long
- 5 faceted clear rondelles, amethyst, (c), 6mm dia. x 4mm long
- 6 round pearls, wine, 5mm dia.
- 18 round pearls, wine, 3mm dia.
- 5 round mother-of-pearl beads, white, (c), 5mm dia.
- 19 freshwater pearls in assorted colors, (h), 5mm dia. x 7mm long: 12 white, 3 light pink, 3 wine, 1 copper
- 2 jump rings, copper, 6mm dia.
- 2 jump rings, copper, 4mm dia.
- 72 crimp beads, copper, 3mm dia.
- Beading wire with nylon coating, mauve, 0.40mm dia.
- 1 hook, copper, 8mm wide x 14mm long
- Masking tape (optional)

TOOLS

- Ruler ■ Wire cutters ■ Crimping pliers
- Chain-nose pliers ■ Bent-nose pliers

Key: (c)= center-drilled; (h)= head-drilled

65

••• Making a Cascade Necklace

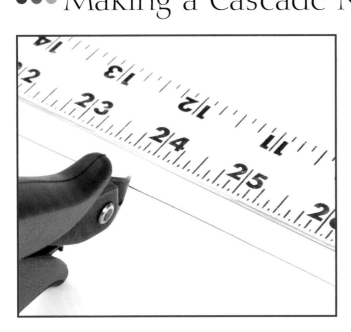

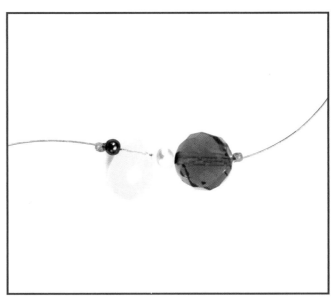

1 Referring to the bead layout (below), lay out the bead groups for each strand on a flat, cloth-covered surface. Then use wire cutters to cut three 24-in. (61.0cm) lengths of beading wire.; set two aside.

2 Referring to strand **A** in the bead layout, thread on one crimp bead, one 3mm wine pearl, one faceted pear-shaped briolette, one white freshwater pearl, one 10mm faceted clear round crystal in root beer, and one crimp bead. Push the beads together.

Bead Layout

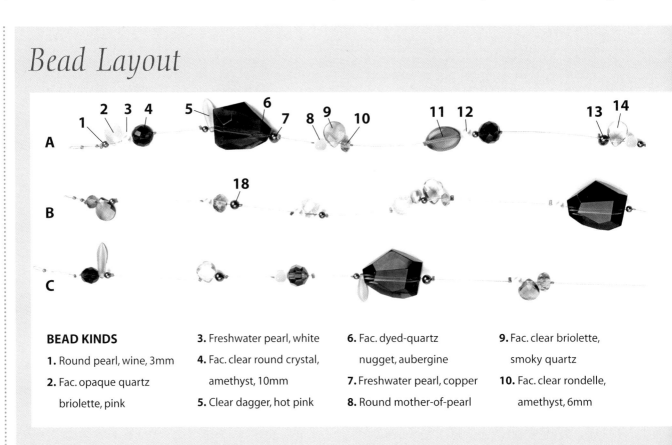

BEAD KINDS

1. Round pearl, wine, 3mm

2. Fac. opaque quartz briolette, pink

3. Freshwater pearl, white

4. Fac. clear round crystal, amethyst, 10mm

5. Clear dagger, hot pink

6. Fac. dyed-quartz nugget, aubergine

7. Freshwater pearl, copper

8. Round mother-of-pearl

9. Fac. clear briolette, smoky quartz

10. Fac. clear rondelle, amethyst, 6mm

3 Use crimping pliers to secure the crimp beads on both sides of the bead group to the beading wire.

4 String the remaining bead groups on strand **A**, threading on a crimp bead before and after each bead group and leaving space between the groups. Secure the crimp beads to the beading wire.

5 Repeat steps 2–4 for strands **B** and **C**. Set all but strand B aside. Trim the end of strand **B** (as shown) to 1 in. (2.5cm). Thread on two crimp beads.

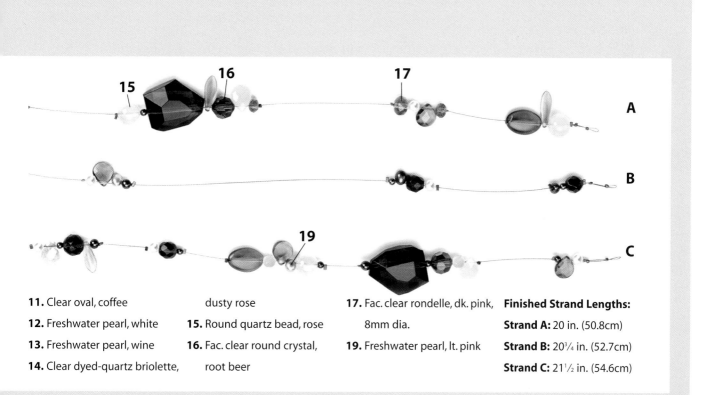

11. Clear oval, coffee

12. Freshwater pearl, white

13. Freshwater pearl, wine

14. Clear dyed-quartz briolette, dusty rose

15. Round quartz bead, rose

16. Fac. clear round crystal, root beer

17. Fac. clear rondelle, dk. pink, 8mm dia.

19. Freshwater pearl, lt. pink

Finished Strand Lengths:

Strand A: 20 in. (50.8cm)

Strand B: 20¾ in. (52.7cm)

Strand C: 21½ in. (54.6cm)

••• Making a Cascade Necklace

6 Fold the wire end in half, making a loop. Thread the Transite end through both crimp beads.

7 Slide the top crimp bead up the wires so that a ⅛-in. (3mm) loop is formed. Use crimping pliers to secure the crimp bead over both thicknesses of wire.

•••helpful tip•••

If you are unsure of the spacing of the bead groups, thread on all beads before securing the crimp beads to the wire. Tape each strand to the work surface, and refer to the bead layout on pages 66 and 67.

10 Open one 6mm jump ring. Thread it through the 4mm jump ring from step 9. Close the jump ring.

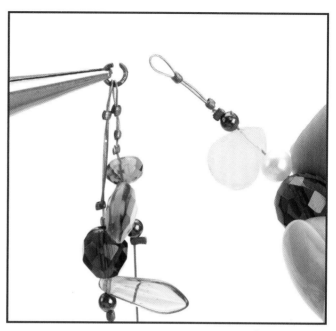

8 Slide the second crimp bead to ½ in. (1.3cm) below the first. Secure the crimp bead over both thicknesses of wire. Repeat the steps to secure the crimp beads on the other end of strand **B**. Then secure the crimp beads on strands **A** and **C**.

9 Open a 4mm jump ring using chain-nose and bent-nose pliers. Referring to the bead layout, match one set of ends on strands **A**, **B**, and **C**, and thread them onto the jump ring; then close the ring.

11 Open one 4mm jump ring. Thread it through the other looped ends of strands **A**, **B**, and **C**; close the jump ring. Open one 6mm jump ring; thread it through the 4mm jump ring and the hook closure. Close the jump ring.

Variation

COMBINATIONS

The combinations of beads with different shapes, cuts, and colors give the "Cascade" necklace its playful elegance. For a necklace of your own design, consider choosing beads in primary colors; mixing beads with frosted and polished finishes; and varying the sizes of the beads.

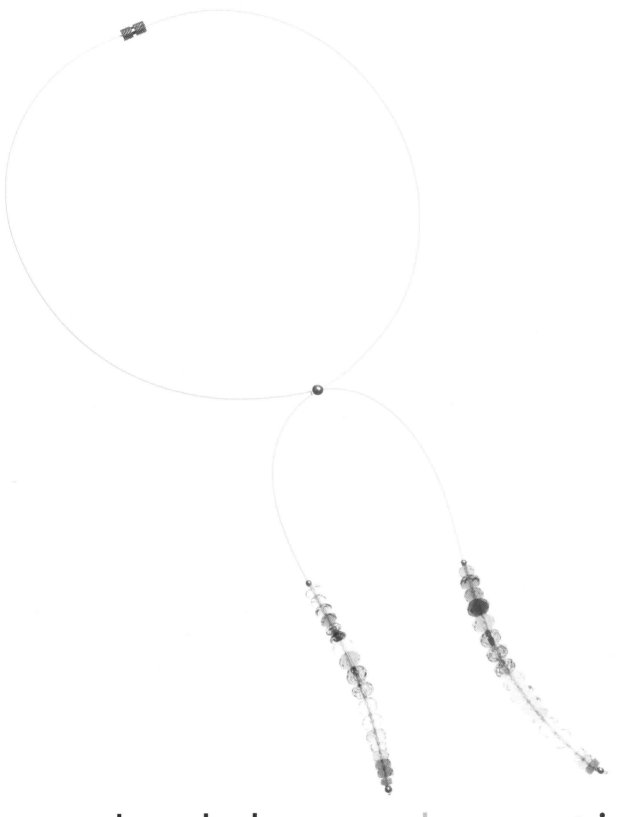

beaded pea pods sprout **in** spring-garden **colors**

Spring Peas

Available in many sizes and colors, rondelles can be stacked in graduated sizes to create these gently tapered pendants. The hues chosen cycle through a rainbow of colors. Strung on resilient beading wire, the weight of the stack of beads causes the tips of the strands to naturally form a gentle curve. Moving the center bead adjusts the necklace opening to complement different neckline styles. If preferred, "Spring Peas" can be worn with one pod hanging lower than the other.

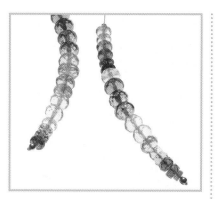

MATERIALS

- Faceted crystal rondelles for small pea pod (in order from bottom of strand):
    1 orange, 4mm dia. x 2mm long
    1 persimmon, 6mm dia. x 3mm long
    1 amber, 6mm dia. x 3mm long
    1 apricot, 6mm dia. x 3mm long
    1 light honey, 6mm dia. x 3mm long
    1 honey, 8mm dia. x 5mm long
    2 citron lemon, 8mm dia. x 5mm long
    1 amber, 8.5mm dia. x 5mm long
    1 madder, 8.5mm dia. x 5mm long
    1 lavender, 8.5mm dia. x 5mm long
    1 clear pink, 8mm dia. x 5mm long
    2 brown, 6mm dia. x 3mm long
    1 chrome green, 7mm dia. x 4mm long
    1 peridot, 7mm dia. x 4mm long
    1 lime, 7mm dia. x 4mm long
    1 sky blue, 7mm dia. x 4mm long
- Faceted crystal rondelles for large pea pod (in order from bottom of strand):
    1 persimmon, 6mm dia. x 3mm long
    1 orange, 6mm dia. x 3mm long
    1 apricot, 6mm dia. x 3mm long
    1 yellow, 7mm dia. x 4mm long
    2 citron lemon, 8mm dia. x 6mm long
    2 honey, 8mm dia. x 4mm long
    2 honey, 9mm dia. x 5mm long
    2 madder, 8.5mm dia. x 5mm long
    2 lavender, 8.5mm dia. x 5mm long
    1 ruby red, 9mm dia. x 6mm long
    2 lavender, 7.5mm dia. x 5mm long
    1 lavender, 6mm dia. x 4mm long
- 1 round bead, sterling-silver, 6mm dia.
- 2 round beads, sterling-silver, 3mm dia.
- 4 crimp beads, silver, 1mm dia., size 2
- 2 crimp-bead covers, sterling-silver, 3mm dia.
- Beading wire, silver-plated, braided, 19 strands, with nylon coating, .024" dia.
- 1 twist-close barrel clasp with thread hole through center, silver, 5mm dia. x 10mm long

TOOLS

- Ruler
- Wire cutters
- Chain-nose pliers
- Crimping pliers
- Bent-nose pliers

Making a Spring Peas Necklace

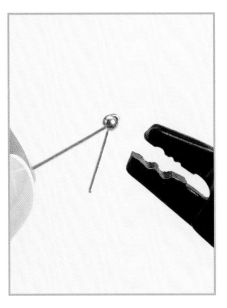

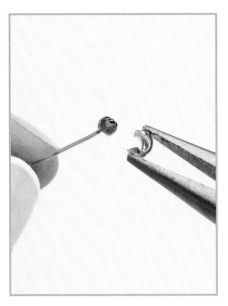

1 Use wire cutters to cut one 17-in. (43.2cm) length and one 18-in. (45.7cm) length of beading wire. Set the 18-in. (45.7cm) length aside.

2 Fold a loop on one end of the 17-in.-long (43.2cm) wire ½ in. (1.3cm) from the end. Slide a crimp bead onto the wire's opposite end and up to the tip of the loop. Use crimping pliers to secure the bead. Cut off the wire tail.

3 Use chain-nose pliers to secure a crimp-bead cover over the crimp bead. Note: the finished end looks like it has a decorative shiny ball on the tip of the wire.

7 Pull the beading wires through the 6mm bead, adjusting the unbeaded lengths of wire above the 6mm bead so that they are long enough to go around the neck.

8 Thread on one-half of the barrel clasp and a crimp bead on one wire end. Bend the wire ½ in. (1.3cm) from the end. Slide the crimp bead to the bend and over the wire end. Use crimping pliers to secure the crimp bead. Trim the wire end using wire cutters.

4 At the other end of the beading wire, thread on the rondelles for the small pea pod in the order specified in the materials list. Tuck the wire end into the beads. Thread on one 3mm silver bead. Set the beaded strand aside.

5 Repeat steps 2–4 for the large pea pod using the 18-in. (45.7cm) length of beading wire set aside in step 1.

6 Thread the ends of the 17-in. (43.2cm) length and the 18-in. (45.7cm) length of beading wires through the hole in the 6mm bead from opposite sides so that they form an "X" with the bead in the center intersection.

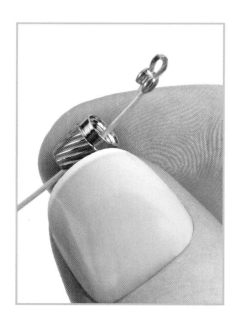

9 Pull on the beading wire, and slide the crimped end into the clasp. Repeat steps 8–9 on the other wire using the second half of the barrel clasp.

Variation

MIXING BEAD FINISHES

Play up the contrast between clear and frosted beads by mixing beads in a smooth tonal range of icy blue and lavender (right). Or mix beads in a range of color with higher contrasts, using beads in amber, honey, pink, fuchsia, and garnet (left).

gleaming ruby crystal and brushed
silver are caught in a play of light

Ruby Drop

A careful juxtaposition of unexpected materials, however humble

or grand, can yield surprisingly refined results. Here, the "Ruby Drop" pendant and necklace display a sophisticated mix of stone, metal, and rubber elements. The pendant is made in a minimal palette—a faceted "ruby" and brushed-silver beads. Suspended from a black cord, the pendant becomes a simple, yet dramatic, piece of jewelry.

MATERIALS

- 1 faceted-quartz nugget, ruby red, 20mm wide x 25mm long x 12mm thick
- 1 oval bead, brushed sterling-silver, 9mm dia. x 33mm long
- 1 round bead, laser-finished sterling-silver, 6mm dia. Note: the finish is also called "stardust."
- 1 round bead, sterling-silver, 3mm dia.
- 1 ring, sterling-silver, 7mm dia. x 2.5mm thick
- 2 tube end caps with rings, sterling-silver, 4mm dia. x 9mm long (including ring) with 3.5mm inner dia.
- 2 jump rings, sterling-silver, 3mm dia.
- 1 magnetic barrel clasp, 4.5mm dia. x 1mm long
- ½ yd. (.46m) hypoallergenic neoprene rubber tubing, black, 3.5mm dia.
- Transite
- Clear household cement

TOOLS

- Ruler
- Utility knife
- Scissors
- Toothpick
- Chain-nose pliers
- Bent-nose pliers
- Cotton swab

••• Making a Ruby Drop Pendant

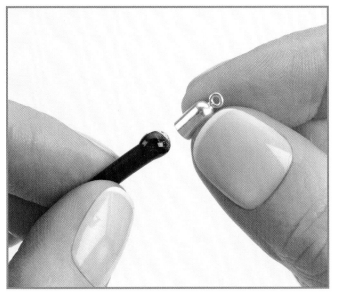

1 Use a utility knife to cut a 15-in. (38.1cm) length of rubber tubing.

2 Coat one end of the tubing with cement. Twist one end cap onto the tubing, and use a cotton swab to immediately wipe off excess cement. Let the cement dry. Repeat on the other end of the tubing.

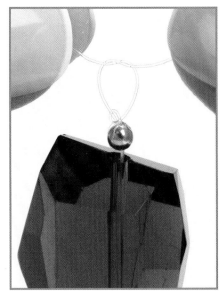

5 Thread both ends of Transite through the oval bead, the 6mm round bead, the ruby nugget, and the 3mm round bead.

6 Thread the Transite ends back into the 3mm round bead at the hole next to the ruby nugget. Pull the Transite through the bead hole. Use a toothpick to slide the bead against the ruby nugget.

7 Leaving a 1/16-in. (1.5mm) space above the silver bead, tie a square knot in the Transite. Add a drop of cement to the knot; let the cement dry. Trim away the excess Transite.

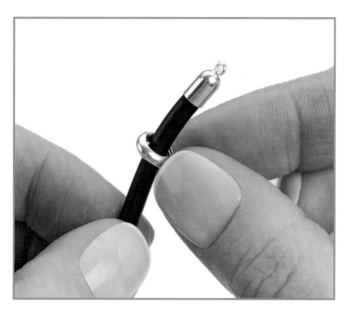

3 Slide the silver ring over the end cap and onto the tubing.

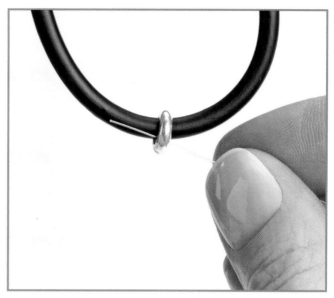

4 Use scissors to cut a10-in. (25.4cm) length of Transite. Thread the Transite through the silver ring, and make the ends even.

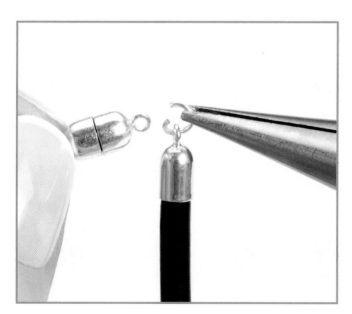

8 Thread an open jump ring through one end cap and the barrel clasp. Use chain-nose and bent-nose pliers to close the jump ring. Repeat at the other end to attach the second half of the barrel clasp.

●●●working tip●●●

End caps increase the diameter of the cord ends. If there is a concern that the silver ring will not fit over the end cap, slide the ring onto the tubing before adhering the end caps.

a pearly starfish appears bathed

Starfish

This charming starfish pendant, with its lustrous pearls and sprinkling of tiny silver glass beads, looks as though it washed up on a moonlit beach. The five-pointed star base—shaped from a single length of wire—is as easily made as drawing a star without lifting the pen. Luminescent pearls are wrapped onto the wire base, and tiny beads that look like a frothy layer of sea foam further embellish the array.

in moonlight

MATERIALS

- 26 round pearls, white, assorted sizes:
  - 1 10mm dia.
  - 5 7mm dia.
  - 5 6mm dia.
  - 5 5mm dia.
  - 10 4mm dia.
- 1 27-g vial no-hole glass micro beads, silver, .5mm dia.
- Wire, sterling-silver, 20 gauge
- Wire, tarnish-resistant, sterling-silver, 28-gauge
- Scrap wire, silver, 24- to 28-gauge
- 18" (45.7cm) omega-chain necklace with magnetic clasp, sterling-silver, approx. 2.5mm dia.

TOOLS

- Ruler
- Wire cutters
- Fine-tip black marker
- Round-nosed pliers
- Chain-nose pliers
- Masking tape
- Denatured alcohol
- Paper towel
- ⅛" (3mm) round stiff-bristle brush
- Extra-thick white tacky glue
- Shallow bowl or saucer
- Cotton swabs

Making a Starfish Pendant

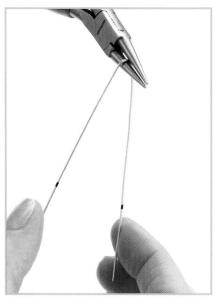

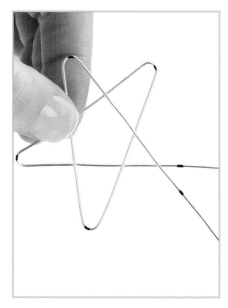

1. Use wire cutters to cut a 12-in. (30.5cm) length of 20-gauge wire. Measuring from one end, use a marker to indicate 1 in. (2.5cm), 3 in. (7.6cm), 5 in. (12.7cm), 7 in. (17.8cm), 9 in. (22.9cm), and 11 in. (27.9cm) on the wire.

2. Place round-nose pliers on the 3-in. (7.6cm) mark. Use your fingers to bend down the wires to make the first arm of the star.

3. Repeat step 2 at marks 5 in. (12.7cm), 7 in. (17.8cm), and 9 in. (22.9cm).

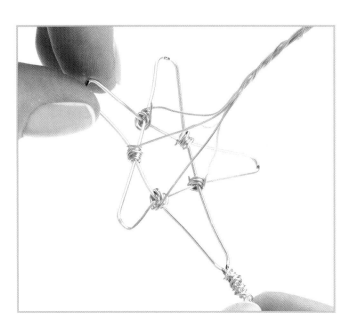

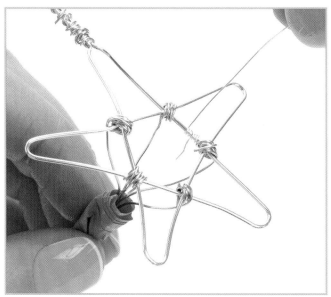

7. Twist the scrap wires together at the center back, and wrap them with masking tape. Remove the marks with alcohol.

8. Cut five 6-in. (15.2cm) lengths of 28-gauge wire. Set four aside. Wrap ¾ in. (1.9cm) of the wire end securely to the center of one side of the pentagon. Bring the wire to the front and *over* the wire of the star.

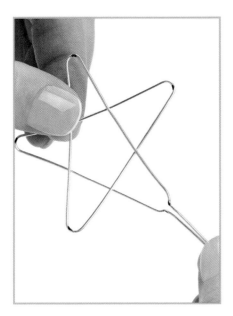

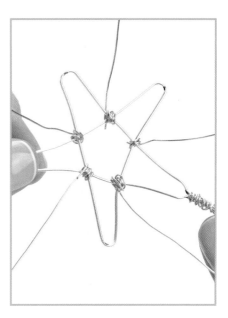

4 At marks 1 in. (2.5cm) and 11 in. (27.9cm), use round-nose pliers to bend the wire ends slightly to form the last arm of the star. Straighten the wire ends. Use chain-nose pliers to pinch the wire ends together.

5 Use scrap wire to bind the wire ends together. Use your fingers to shape the star, tapering the arms and curving them slightly so that the front of the star is slightly dome shaped.

6 Cut five 6-in. (15.2cm) lengths of scrap wire. Use them to bind each corner of the pentagon at the center of the star.

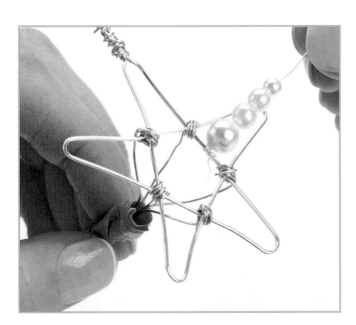

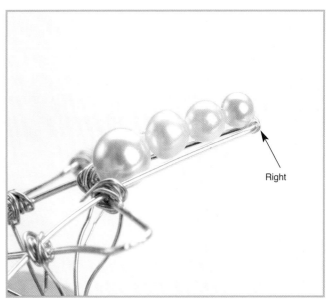

Right

9 Thread the pearls on the wire, one each of 7mm, 6mm, 5mm, and 4mm. Thread them in decreasing size as shown.

10 Anchor the pearls by wrapping the wire *over* and around the tip of the star, bringing it to the underside, and then up through the inside of the star to the right of the 4mm pearl (indicated on the photo by an arrow).

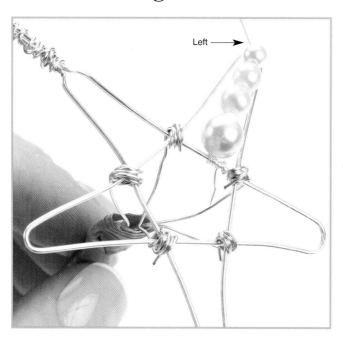

Left ⟶

11 Wrap the wire over the end of the star, around to the underside, and up through the inside of the star to the left of the 4mm pearl (indicated on the photo by an arrow).

12 Bring the wire across the back to the right of the star, then up and over the star, wrapping the wire between the 4mm and 5mm pearls. Continue to wrap the wire between the remaining pearls. Secure the wire end to the starting point.

15 To add the 4mm pearls at each corner of the pentagon, wrap the wire to the nearest corner; thread on a 4mm pearl; and wrap the wire to the same corner. Do not cut the wire. Repeat at each corner. Cut off the excess wire at the last corner.

16 Remove the scrap wire from the star's tail ends. Use round-nose pliers to bend the tail ends to the back to form a hook. Grasp the wire ends with round-nose pliers, and roll the wire up. Cut a 4-in. (10.2cm) length of 28-gauge wire, and wrap a portion of the hook, as shown.

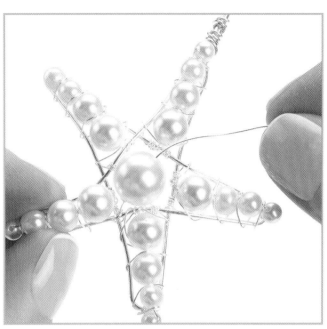

13 Repeat steps 8–13 to attach the pearls to the remaining arms. Note: the thin wire should wrap over the star wire so that the pearls remain on the top plane of the star.

14 Cut off the bindings and bundled scrap wires from steps 6–7. Cut a 6-in. (15.2cm) length of 28-gauge wire. Wrap ¾ in. (1.9cm) of the wire end to and over one corner of the pentagon. Thread on a 10mm pearl. Wrap the wire end to and over the center of the opposite side of the pentagon.

17 Brush a thin coat of glue on the sides of the arms. When the glue is tacky, place the star in a bowl, and apply the micro beads to the glued areas, swooshing the beads to fill in any crevices; let the glue dry. Repeat for center of the star, using the brush to reach all of the crevices. Let the glue dry.

18 Allow the star to dry thoroughly. Thread a chain through the hook on the pendant.

a plump pink pearl nestles
in a golden swing

Infinity

The "Infinity" pendant is made by weaving a peyote-beaded strip, giving it a twist, and joining the ends to make a loop. This clever design is based on the Möbius strip that was discovered by mathematician August Ferdinand Möbius in 1858. Nestled in the bottom curve of the strip is a lustrous pearl that picks up the color of the golden loop that cradles it. The design is suited to beginning weavers because the technique is straightforward and yields a high-end look.

MATERIALS

- 1 4-gram tube (approx. 800 beads) Delica seed beads, 24kt bright gold-plated, size 11/0 (Note: approx. 375 beads are needed.)
- 1 bobbin nonmetallic Nymo nylon thread, gold, size B
- 1 round pearl, pale pink, 10mm dia.
- Transite
- Cyanoacrylate (instant glue)
- 18" (45.7cm) round hollow-mesh chain, sterling-silver, 5mm dia.
- 2 end caps with rings, silver, 5mm inside dia. x 6mm long (9mm long with rings)
- 2 jump rings, silver, 5mm dia.
- 1 lobster clasp, silver

TOOLS

- Scissors
- Beading needle, #10
- Ruler
- Wire cutters
- Round-nose pliers
- Chain-nose pliers
- Bent-nose pliers

••• Making an Infinity Pendant

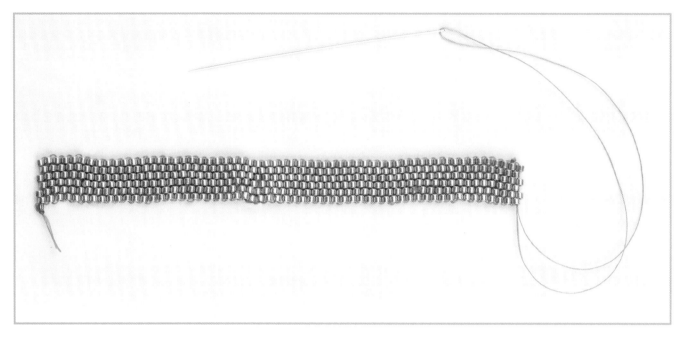

1 To begin, read "Weaving Beads" on pages 152 to 157. String a stopper bead onto a double strand of thread 24 in. (61.0cm) long. Row 1: string on six gold beads. Continue beading rows until the strip is 3½ in. (8.9cm) long. Note: do not cut off the needle.

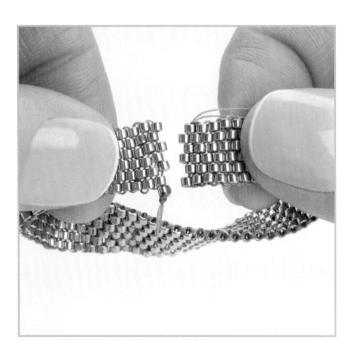

3 Bring the ends of the strip together. Note: the two ends should match. If they don't interlock, add another row of beads.

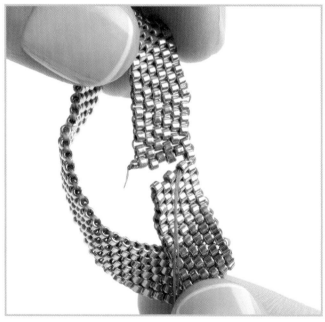

4 Insert the needle through the first bead on the opposite edge; then continue alternating the beads of the first and last rows to secure them together. End on the same side of the strip as the stopper bead. Cut the needle from the thread.

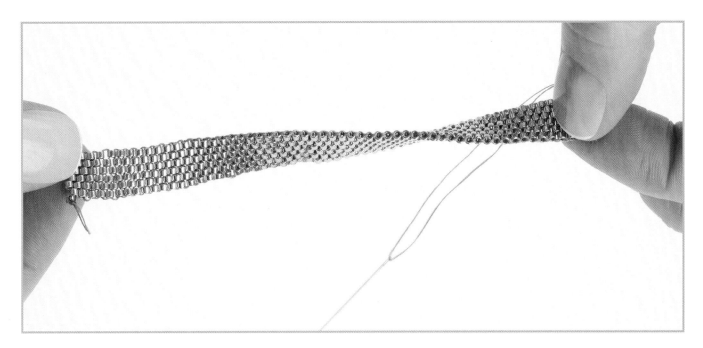

2 Hold the ends of the strip, and twist the strip.

5 Use a needle to open the knot next to the stopper bead.
Remove the stopper bead. Working close to the last bead,
tie the weaving ends and the stopper-bead ends together into a
square knot. Apply a drop of glue; let it dry; and trim the thread.

Ready-Made Chain

A purchased silver-mesh
chain, complete with end
caps and clasp, can be
used instead of putting the
chain together yourself.
Because the chain is a hollow tube, it is lightweight
and relatively inexpensive,
even in sterling silver.

Making an Infinity Pendant

design tip

Because the Möbius strip is flexible, it will have a different appearance depending on the thickness of the chain. Try different chain diameters when shopping for ready-made chain. On thin chain, the strip will slump into an elongated shape. On thick chain, it will open into a wider figure-eight shape.

6 The finished Möbius-style pendant should look like this. It should have smooth even rows and columns of beads with no messy loops of thread.

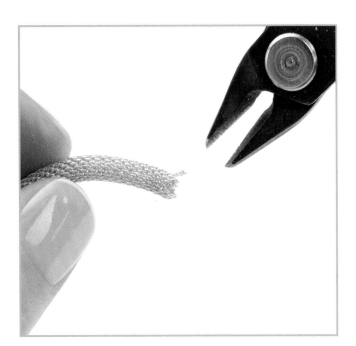

9 Use wire cutters to cut a 16-in. (40.6cm) length of chain. Trim the frayed or uneven edges. Insert a jaw of the round-nose pliers into the chain, and rotate it to smooth the inner wall.

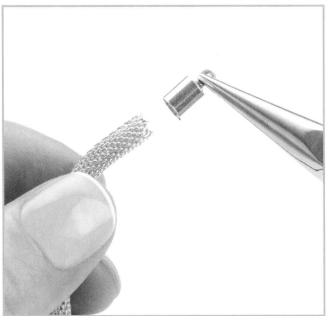

10 Apply a drop of glue to one end of the chain. Insert the chain end into the end cap. Let the glue dry. Repeat on the other end with the remaining end cap.

7 Center the pearl on a 6-in. (15.2cm) length of Transite. Insert the Transite ends through the strip from the inside, one row apart, centering the pearl on the joining seam.

8 Secure the pearl by tying the Transite ends into a square knot. Apply a drop of glue; let it dry; and trim the ends. Set the piece aside.

11 Use chain-nose and bent-nose pliers to open one jump ring. Thread it through one end-cap ring and a lobster clasp. Close the jump ring. Attach the remaining jump ring to the other end.

12 Thread the chain through the pendant, centering it when wearing the necklace. (The back view of the pendant is shown; for the front view, see page 84.)

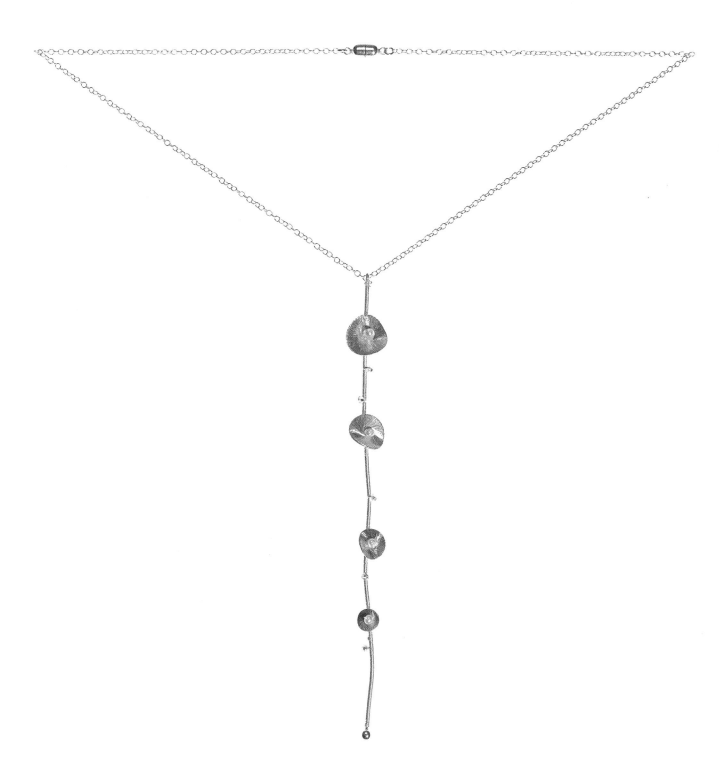

bright gold disks **with pearl**
droplets **accent a** silver stem

Water Lily

A luxurious combination of bright silver and brushed-gold vermeil is garnished with delicate freshwater pearls and faceted beads on this elegantly elongated pendant. The "Water Lily" pendant looks particularly dramatic worn over dark velvet or other matte-fabric garments, which bring out the luster of the metals as well as the sparkle of the crystal. Although the pendant looks like a complicated piece to make, it is as easy as any wire-wrapping project.

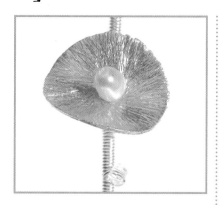

MATERIALS

- 4 "warped" spacer beads, brushed gold vermeil, in assorted sizes:
  - 1 12mm dia.
  - 1 10mm dia.
  - 1 8mm dia.
  - 1 6mm dia.
- 4 freshwater pearls, white, in assorted sizes:
  - 1 3mm dia.
  - 3 2mm dia.
- 5 clear Austrian-crystal beads, 1.5mm dia.
- Wire, silver-plated with copper core, 20-gauge
- Wire, silver, 28-gauge
- Transite
- 1 half-drilled round memory-wire end bead, silver, 3mm dia.
- 16" (40.6cm) of cable-link chain, silver, 1mm dia. links
- 2 jump rings, silver, 3mm dia.
- 1 oval magnetic clasp, silver, 4.5mm dia. x 12mm long

TOOLS

- Ruler
- Wire cutters
- Round-nose pliers
- Chain-nose pliers
- Bent-nose pliers
- Cyanoacrylate gel (instant glue)

Making a Water Lily Pendant

1 Use wire cutters to cut a 5-in. (12.7cm) length of 20-gauge wire for the stem.

2 Use the very tip of the round-nose pliers to make a loop with a $\frac{1}{16}$-in. (1.5mm) inside diameter at one end. Set it aside.

3 Cut four 4-in. (10.2cm) lengths of Transite. Thread one length from the back of the 12mm spacer bead through the 3mm pearl, and back through the hole in the spacer bead. Note: the Transite ends should be equal lengths on the back of the spacer bead.

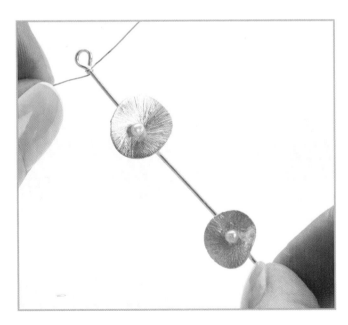

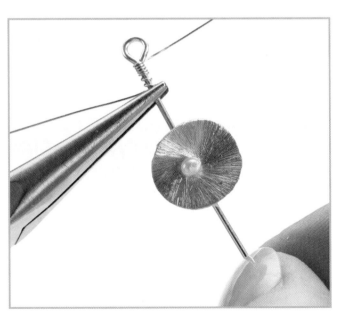

6 Have the spacer beads face in one direction. Cut a 48-in. (1.2m) length of 28-gauge silver wire. Leaving a $\frac{3}{4}$-in. tail and beginning under the loop, wrap the stem with silver wire.

7 Continue wrapping the stem tightly and evenly with wire. Use chain-nose pliers to slide the wire wraps together to eliminate any spaces between the wire wraps.

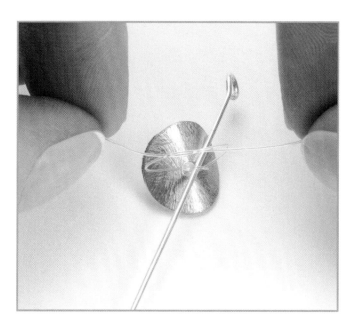

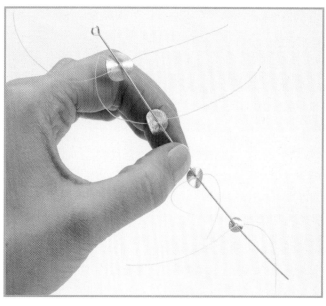

4 Place the wire on your work surface with the loop at the top. Position the spacer bead from step 3 ³⁄₄ in. (1.9cm) from the base of the loop. Make two square knots in the Transite to tie the spacer bead to the wire.

5 Using 2mm pearls, repeat steps 3–4 for the remaining spacer beads. Tie the spacer beads to the wire in order of descending size. Leave 1 in. (2.5cm) between the 12mm and 10mm spacer beads, and between the 10mm and 8mm spacer beads. Leave ³⁄₄ in. (1.9cm) between the 8mm and 6mm spacer beads. Trim the ends to ¹⁄₄ in. (6mm).

Neat Wire Wraps

For the easiest and neatest wire-wrapping, keep the 20-gauge wire (stem) straight. Once wrapping the stem is complete, it can be manipulated into bends. Because the bends are so slight, no gaps will be seen between the wire wraps.

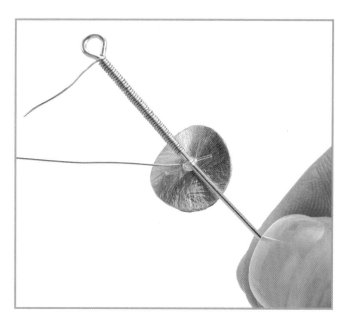

8 Wrap the wire to within ¹⁄₄ in. (3mm) of the knot of the first spacer bead. Bend pressing it against the stem wire; then continue wrapping the wire to conceal it.

Making a Water Lily Pendant

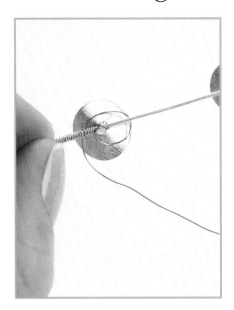

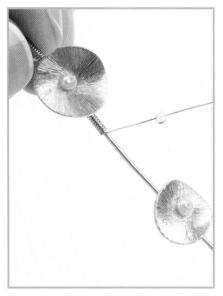

9 Wrap the wire in an "X" across the knot. Then wrap the wire in a full circle under the spacer. Continue to wrap the wire down the stem in the same radial direction as before, neatly concealing the second Transite tail under the wire wraps.

10 Wrap the stem for approximately ¼ in. (6mm) below the bottom rim of the spacer. Thread the crystal bead onto the silver wire. Note: the crystals will all face in slightly different directions.

11 Continue wrapping down the stem for another ¼ in. (6mm). Thread on another crystal bead. Repeat steps 7–11 to the end of the stem, positioning one crystal ½ in. (1.3cm) below the 10mm gold spacer, one crystal ⅛ in. (3mm) below the 8mm gold spacer, and one crystal ⅛ in. (3mm) below the 6mm gold spacer.

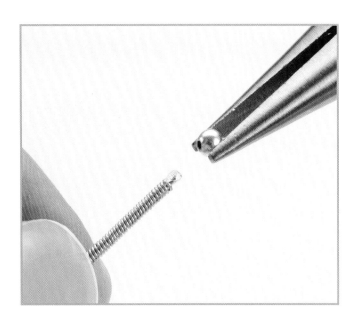

13 Apply a drop of glue to the bottom of the stem wire. Push the memory-wire end bead onto the stem end. Let the glue dry.

14 With the top loop facing front to back and the spacers facing forward, use your fingers to gently curve the stem to the left and to the right as shown. Wrap the wire tail (from step 6) to conceal the gap in the top loop; then trim and press the wire end neatly against the stem.

Findings rarely play featured roles in jewelry design, but in "Water Lily" spacer beads are central to the lithe elegance of the pendant. For the same finished look, orient each pearl so that its holes are horizontal and it sits over the hole in the spacer bead so the pearl's "good" side faces outward.

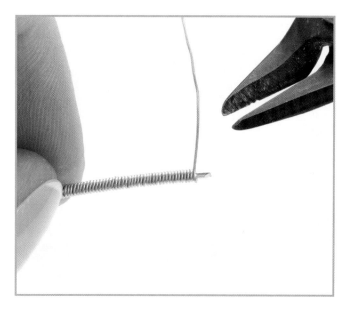

12 Leave a scant ¹⁄₁₆ in. (1.6mm) of the stem end unwrapped. Trim away any excess silver wire. Use chain-nose pliers to press the wire end flush against the stem.

15 Thread one end of the chain through the loop of the finished pendant, and slide the pendant to the center of the chain. Note: the pendant will face forward and the bends will go from side to side.

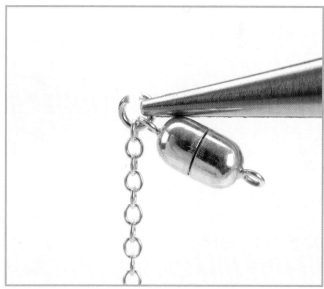

16 Use chain-nose and bent-nose pliers to open a jump ring. Thread the jump ring through one end of the chain and the magnetic-clasp loop. Close the jump ring. Repeat at the other end of the chain using the remaining jump ring.

pick a lush harvest of color—
cherry, grapefruit, and orange

Deco Harvest

The deliciously fruity colors of these beads resemble the cherry and orange colors of Bakelite, the first synthetic plastic developed in 1909. Here, "Deco Harvest" recreates the prized look of Bakelite jewelry using ordinary rondelle, oval, and round beads in suitable vintage colors. When the beads in dyed quartz and translucent finishes are paired with glass flowers, berries, and leaves, the resulting design is a convincing reproduction of the sought-after originals.

MATERIALS

- 1 faceted translucent dyed-quartz rondelle, celadon, 14mm dia. x 9mm long
- 2 faceted translucent dyed-quartz round beads, 10mm dia.:
  - 1 pink grapefruit
  - 1 lemon
- 1 faceted opaque dyed-quartz rondelle, cherry red, 19mm dia. x 14mm long
- 1 opaque dyed-quartz round bead, orange, 15mm dia.
- 3 transparent glass flower beads, 10mm dia. x 4mm thick:
  - 1 goldenrod
  - 1 olive
  - 1 amber
- 1 frosted-glass leaf, olive, 10mm wide x 30mm long x 2mm thick
- 3 oval beads, brushed gold, 4mm dia. x 8mm long
- 5 crimp beads*, gold, 1mm dia. (*used without crimping)
- 5 headpins with 2mm ball end, gold:
  - 1 3" (76mm) long
  - 1 2½" (64mm) long
  - 3 2" (51mm) long
- 2 jump rings, gold, 4mm dia.
- Wire, gold, 24-gauge
- 21" (53.3cm) long cable-link chain necklace, silk-thread covered, olive green, 6-mm dia. links

TOOLS

- Ruler
- Chain-nose pliers
- Round-nose pliers
- Bent-nose pliers
- Wire cutters
- Emery cloth, 200-grit and 400-grit (optional)

1 Flatten the glass flowers as described below. Thread the olive flower, orange bead, round gold bead, and oval gold bead on a 2½-in.-long (6.4cm) headpin.

2 Use chain-nose pliers to grasp the headpin ¼ in. (6.0mm) from the top bead. Turn the pliers away from you to bend the wire at a 90-deg. angle.

3 Use round-nose pliers to grasp the headpin wire ⅛ in. (3.0mm) from the bend. Rotate the pliers toward the bend.

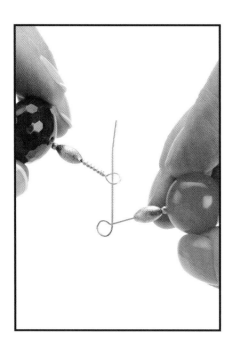

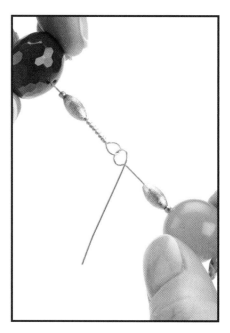

Flattening a Glass Flower

Moisten 200-grit emery cloth with water, and place it—abrasive side up—on a protected work surface. With your fingertip on top, place the flower's back on the emery cloth. Rub the back of the flower on the emery cloth until the flower's back has flattened. Then switch to a moistened 400-grit emery cloth to create a smoother finish; then wipe off the dust.

7 Insert the wire that extends from the orange-bead unit (from step 4) through the loop on the cherry-red bead unit.

8 Slide the orange-bead unit along the wire until both bead units are connected at their loops.

4 Use your fingers to bend the wire around one jaw of the pliers, crossing the wire in front to make a loop; set the orange-bead unit aside. Note: do not finish wrapping the wire around the stem.

5 Thread the goldenrod flower, the red rondelle, the round gold bead, and the oval gold bead on a 3-in.-long (7.6cm) headpin. Make a wrapped loop ½ in. (1.3cm) from the top bead as in steps 2–4.

6 Wrap the wire around the stem to complete the cherry-red bead unit. Refer to the table (below) for the finished length.

finished lengths of bead units

BEAD UNIT	LENGTH
Pink Grapefruit	¾" (1.9cm)
Orange	1⅜" (3.5cm)
Cherry Red	1⅝" (4.1cm)
Celadon	1⅛" (2.8cm)
Lemon	¾" (1.9cm)

The different lengths of the bead units allow the pieces of "fruit" to hang in a cluster without obscuring any one of them.

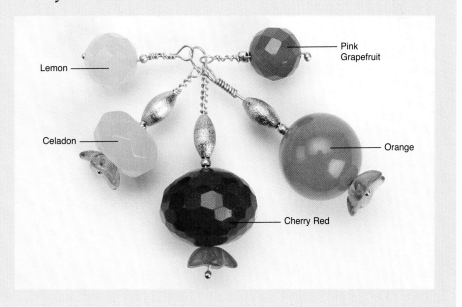

Lemon

Celadon

Pink Grapefruit

Orange

Cherry Red

Making a Deco Harvest Pendant

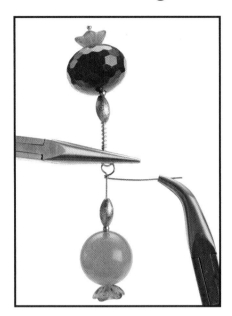

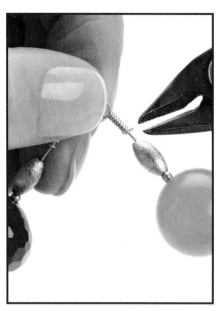

9 Use chain-nose and bent-nose pliers to wrap the wire on the orange-bead unit around the headpin to form a loop.

10 Continue to wrap the wire around and down the headpin to complete the wrapped loop on the orange-bead unit. Use wire cutters to trim away any excess wire.

11 Use chain-nose pliers to squeeze the cut end of the wire flush against the headpin stem on the orange-bead unit.

variation

FANTASY FRUIT

Using color combinations not ordinarily found in nature gives the pendant high style. Pair tiny flowers in pale blue, lavender, and aqua with larger beads (shown right); then suspend the cluster from a delicate gold chain.

15 Cut a 3-in. (7.6cm) length of gold wire. Follow the directions on page 164 to make a wrapped loop on the green leaf. Use chain-nose and bent-nose pliers to thread an open jump ring through the leaf's loop and the loop on the bead assembly completed in step 14. Close the jump ring.

12 Thread a pink-grapefruit bead and a round gold bead onto a 2-in.-long (5.1cm) headpin. Follow steps 2–4 and 7–11 to make a pink-grapefruit-bead unit according to the size in the table, and attach it to the loop on the red-and-orange-bead assembly.

13 Thread an amber flower, celadon rondelle, round gold bead, and oval gold bead onto a 2-in.-long (5.1cm) headpin. Follow steps 2–4 and 7–11 to make a bead unit; attach it to the loop on the completed bead assembly.

14 Thread the lemon bead and the round gold bead on a 2-in.-long (5.1cm) headpin. Follow steps 2–4 and 7–11 to make a bead unit, and attach it to the loop on the bead assembly made in step 13.

●● helpful tip ●●

Glass flowers are usually tiny, but sometimes they have protruding backs that keep them from lying flush against the beads that are strung next to them. To modify unsuitable flowers, simply use emery cloth to smooth the backs of the flowers, referring to "Flattening a Glass Flower" on page 98 for general directions.

16 Thread an open jump ring through the loop on the completed bead assembly and the center link of the chain. Close the jump ring.

a simple brooch has
double-feature glamour

Classic Acorns

Reminiscent of 1930s Hollywood, this charming all-in-one brooch and pendant has two "acorns" cleverly assembled from oval smoky-topaz beads, and caps made from findings. Together with ribbon, the design elements complete the illusion of jeweled acorns dangling from a velvet bow. Whether the vintage, retro-chic acorns are pinned to a coat like a brooch or hang like a pendant from a velvet choker, "Classic Acorns" has ultra glam-girl style.

MATERIALS

- 2 oval quartz beads, brown-gray, 17mm dia. x 21mm long
- 1 flat-back pearl, green, 8mm dia.
- 1 electroplated oak leaf, gunmetal, 34mm wide x 51mm long x 0.75mm thick
- 2 bead caps, any color, 18mm dia. x 7mm thick
- 2 metal rings, any color, 18mm dia. x 3mm thick
- 2 headpins with 2mm ball end, silver, 26-gauge, 3" (7.6cm) long
- 1 stickpin with pad, silver, 2¼" (5.7cm) long
- 1 yd. (0.9m) round elastic cord, dark brown, 1mm dia.
- Velvet ribbon, loden green, ⅝" (15mm) wide:
    - ¼ yd. (0.23m) (for ribbon bow)
    - ½ yd. (0.46m) (optional: for choker-style necklace pendant)
- Matching sewing thread

TOOLS

- Toothpicks
- Cyanoacrylate (instant glue)
- Scissors
- Extra-thick white tacky glue
- Pointed tweezers
- ¼-in.-wide (6mm) flat-bristle brush
- Round-nose pliers
- Wire cutters
- Ruler
- Hand-sewing needle

••• Making a Classic Acorns Pendant

1 Insert a toothpick into the hole in one bead cap; set one half aside. Place one metal ring on your work surface. Coat the top and sides with instant glue. Glue the bead cap to the ring; let the glue dry.

2 Cut the elastic cord in half; set one half aside. Use a toothpick to apply a small amount of craft glue adjacent to the hole in the bead cap. Using tweezers, adhere the elastic end to the glue, allowing $\frac{1}{8}$ in. (1.5mm) to extend beyond the hole; let the glue dry.

4 Continue to adhere the cord to the bead cap until it is covered to its outer rim. Do not cut the cord. Note: use your finger and firm pressure to "set" the cord onto the cap as you work.

5 Turn the cap over. Test-fit the cap on the bead to determine how many rows of cord are needed to conceal the ring. Apply glue to the metal ring; then position and adhere the cord. Trim the cord, leaving a 1-in. (2.5cm) end. Glue the end inside the bead cap.

●●●helpful tip●●●

For the acorn cap to fit snugly on the bead, its center must be as perfectly round as possible. Some glass beads can be lumpy, so choose those that are smooth and round at one end.

3 Use the brush to coat the bead cap with a thin layer of craft glue. Adhere the cord to the bead cap in even rows by rotating the toothpick. Apply more glue as needed. Be careful not to get the glue on the face of the cord.

6 Insert one headpin through a quartz bead and a covered bead cap.

7 Use round-nose pliers to make an eye loop close to the bead cap. Trim off any excess wire. Repeat steps 1–7 to make a second acorn.

8 Cut two 4-in. (10.2cm) lengths from the remaining elastic cord. Set one aside. Fold one length in half, and thread both ends through the eye loop. Insert the ends through the loop in the cord, and pull them tight. Hold the ends together, and tie them using an overhand knot. Pull the knot tight, and trim the ends. Repeat step 8 for the second acorn.

9 Tie 3³/₄-in.-wide (9.5cm) bow using the velvet ribbon. Loosen the bow, and insert the tweezers behind the center loop. Grasp the elastic cord on one acorn using tweezers, and pull the cord to the opposite side of the loop. Repeat with the second acorn.

11 Secure the elastic ends by making stitches under the loop of the bow knot. With the bow wrong side up, sew the stem of the leaf to the center back of the bow.

12 Trim the bow tails to ³/₄ in. (1.9cm). Fold the edge of one tail up and over the top of the leaf and the stitches, and sew it to the back of the bow knot. Repeat with the other tail. Set the assembly aside. Optional: to make a pendant, do not follow steps 13 and 14. Refer to "Acorn Pendant," opposite top, for general directions.

10 Tighten the velvet bow, trapping the elastics on the acorns within the center loop.

Acorn Pendant

To convert the brooch into a pendant for a choker-style necklace, follow all but steps 13 and 14 in the directions. Securley stitch the back of the bow knot (completed in step 12) to the center of the right side of the 18-in.-long (45.7cm) velvet ribbon. Tie the ribbon ends together at the back of your neck.

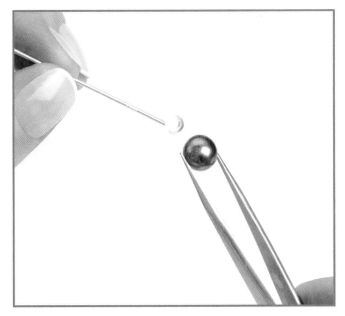

13 Using instant glue, adhere the flat side of the pearl to the pad end of the stick pin.

14 Turn the bow to the right side. Position the stick pin as desired.

dangling faceted stones glisten
like sunlit southern seas

Caribbean Waters

The exquisitely simple design of these earrings relies not only on

their striking shape but on the singularly glorious color of the blue indicolite cut crystals that are placed for maximum impact. Making the earrings doesn't require extra hardware—the beads hang on their own stem wires, and Smart Beads seat themselves so that the stones do not need to be crimped in place. The spare design combines few elements but makes a dramatic and sophisticated statement.

MATERIALS

- 2 indicolite crystal nuggets, aqua blue, 13mm wide x 16mm long x 9mm thick
- 2 faceted dyed-quartz briolettes, teardrop shape, peridot green, 7.5mm dia. x 12mm long
- Wire, sterling-silver, 20-gauge
- Wire, sterling-silver, 24-gauge
- 2 round Smart Beads, sterling-silver, 4mm dia.

TOOLS

- Ruler
- Wire cutters
- Needle file
- Emery cloth, 400-grit
- Fine-tip black marker
- Round-nose pliers
- Chain-nose pliers
- Rubbing alcohol
- Paper towel

Making Caribbean Waters Earrings

1 Use wire cutters to cut two 4-in. (10.2cm) lengths of 20-gauge wire. Deburr one end of each wire using a needle file. Use emery cloth to polish the ends until they are rounded. Note: the polished and shaped ends will be inserted into pierced ears, so give them extra attention.

2 Use the very tip of the round-nose pliers to make a small eye loop in the shape of a tapered teardrop in the unpolished end of each wire. Leave the loop slightly open.

6 Mark a point at 1³/₄-in. (4.4cm) above the Smart Bead on each wire. Use your fingertips to gently make a bend in each wire at the mark. Then test-fit the earrings, making sure they hang upright.

●● helpful tip ●●

To check that your earrings hang straight, rest the bends of the ear wires over a thin rod, such as a pencil. If the earrings hang backward, they are off balance; they will need to be fixed or they will not hang right on your earlobes. To straighten the earrings, carefully use the tip of the needle-nose pliers just above the Smart Beads to bend the Indicolite beads slightly forward a few degrees so that the assemblies hang upright.

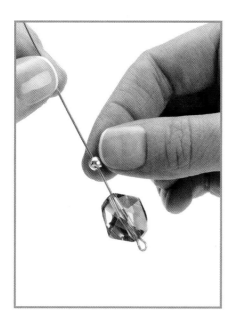

3 Thread one crystal nugget and one Smart Bead onto each wire, sliding them all the way down to the eye loop. Set the bead assemblies aside.

4 Use wire cutters to cut two 3½-in. (8.9cm) lengths of 24-gauge wire. Set one aside. Follow the directions on page 165 to make a wrapped loop on one peridot briolette. Repeat with the second briolette and the remaining wire.

5 Thread the briolettes onto the eye loops; close the eye loops.

variation

CREATING AN ORIGINAL

The size, shape, color, and movement of the design elements in "Caribbean Waters"—the large chunky cut of the indicolite vs. the slender and smooth teardrop shape of the brio-lette; the zingy hot aqua vs. the softer peridot green; and the stationary indicol-ite stone vs. the swing of the briolette—are balanced to appealing effect.

Design Tip

Smart Beads greatly simp-lify many projects in which crimp beads might otherwise be used. They slide onto wire and stay put due to an inner silicone liner that grips the wire securely. Used in place of the crimp bead or crimp tube, they give jewelry a more finished look because they don't have the seams found on crimp beads.

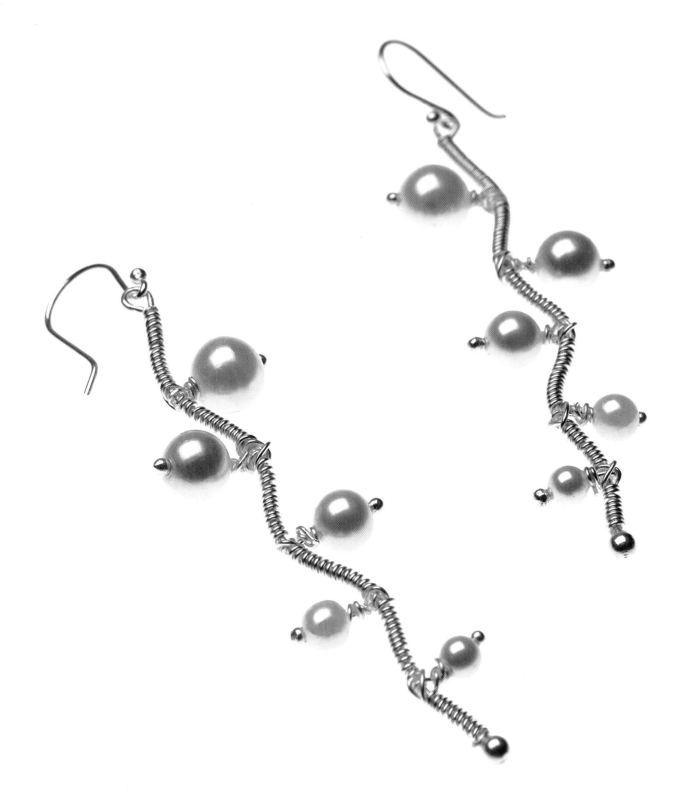

fun little rivulets of silver carry
pretty pearls along their bends

Zigzag

Pearls in graduated sizes can be threaded onto a strand to make earrings with a classic look, but why not try something more adventurous? Combine pearls and wire in a restrained monochromatic palette, using a unique and easy wrapping technique to create earrings with contemporary flair. Five beautiful pearls in graduated size are secured to a thick base wire, which is then wrapped with thin wire and bent into sensual curves on these artful "Zigzag" earrings.

MATERIALS

- *10 round pearls, natural, assorted sizes:*
    - *2 8mm dia.*
    - *2 7mm dia.*
    - *2 6mm dia.*
    - *2 5mm dia.*
    - *2 4mm dia.*
- *Wire, sterling-silver, 20-gauge*
- *Wire, tarnish-resistant sterling-silver, 24-gauge*
- *10 headpins with 2mm ball end, sterling-silver, 26-gauge, 1½" (3.8cm) long*
- *2 half-drilled round memory-wire end beads, sterling-silver, 3mm dia. (Note: the inner dia. of the hole must accommodate 20-gauge wire.)*
- *1 pair fish-hook ear wires with ball end, sterling-silver*

TOOLS

- *Ruler*
- *Wire cutters*
- *Needle file*
- *Emery cloth, 400-grit*
- *Dowel, ⁵⁄₈" (15mm) dia.*
- *Masking tape*
- *Round-nose pliers*
- *Cyanoacrylate gel (instant glue)*
- *Chain-nose pliers*
- *Bent-nose pliers*

Making Zigzag Earrings

  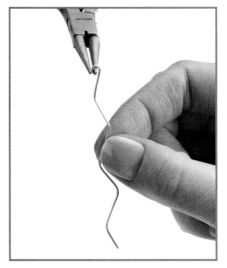

1. Use wire cutters to cut two 3-in. (7.6cm) lengths of 20-gauge wire. Smooth the wire ends using a needle file and then an emery cloth. Set the wires aside. Tape the dowel to a flat work surface.

2. To make zigzags, position the end of one wire over the dowel; press down on both sides with equal pressure to bend the wire; turn the wire over. Move down the wire from the bend, and position the wire over the dowel; press down on both sides. Continue along the wire until five bends in opposite directions are made.

3. Repeat step 2 with the second wire. Use the ball of your thumb to smooth the wave shape on the wires. Turn the wires to their sides to ensure that they are flat. Then use the very tip of the round-nose pliers to make a 1/16-in. (1.5mm) eye loop at the top of each wire.

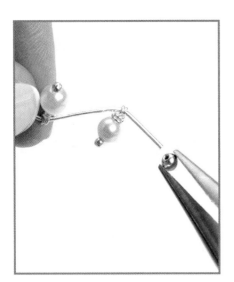 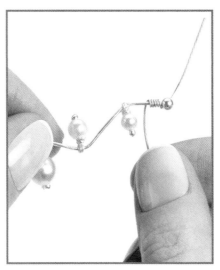 

7. Apply a drop of glue to the bottom end of one zigzag wire. Insert the end into an end bead. Repeat for the second zigzag wire. Let the glue dry.

8. Cut two 15-in. (38.1cm) lengths of 24-gauge wire; set one aside. Leaving a 1-in. (2.5cm) end for leverage, position the wire at the bottom of one zigzag wire, and wrap the wire as close to one side of the pearl as possible. When no more wire can be wound, bring the wire to the pearl's back.

9. Bring the wire under the pearl, and continue to wrap the wire on the other side of the pearl. Don't change the direction of the wrap. Wrap up to the eye loop. Trim off both ends of wrapping wire. Use bent-nose pliers to squeeze the cut ends against the zigzag. Repeat steps 8–9 for the second earring.

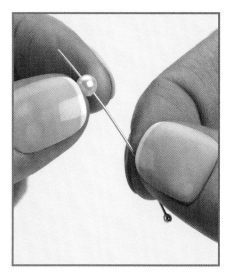

4 Thread one 4mm pearl onto a head-pin.

5 Place the headpin against the zigzag wire so that the pearl is positioned in the first bend from the bottom. Leave $\frac{1}{8}$ in. (3mm) of the headpin stem between the pearl and the wire. Wrap the headpin tightly twice around the wire and around the headpin stem above the pearl until the gap is filled. Trim off any excess wire.

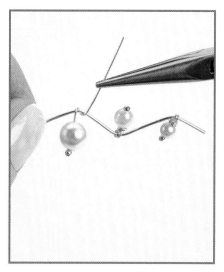

6 Repeat steps 4–5 to attach the pearls in increasing sizes in each bend. Repeat for the second zigzag wire.

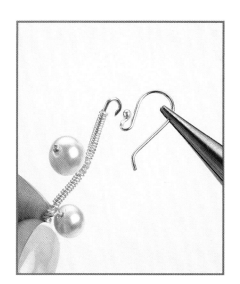

10 Place the earrings on your work surface. Have the zigzags mirror each other. Use chain-nose pliers to secure the ear wires, opening the eye loops if necessary.

variation

SOFT COLORWAYS

Turn the understated design of the "Zigzag" earrings into one that is less subtle. Instead of the monochromatic palette of the originals, use graduated pearls in a mix of soft pastels, such as rose, lavender, gray, and moss green.

a classic design pairs
simple elements with bright
glitter and subtle glow

Les Anciennes

The tasteful
combination of
small interesting
shapes in the

"Les Anciennes" earrings lends classic
style to these beaded creations. The earrings feature cubic-zirconium crystals
in the shape of keystones with long
vertical facets that refract light without
overpowering the soft glow of the
brushed matte finish of the gold disks.
Small freshwater pearls on delicate
loops connect the design elements and
play out the ancient mix of gold, fuchsia, and citron colors.

Making Les Anciennes Earrings

1 Use wire cutters to cut two 3-in. (7.6cm) lengths of wire. Set one aside. Then read "Caution" (below) before proceeding to step 2.

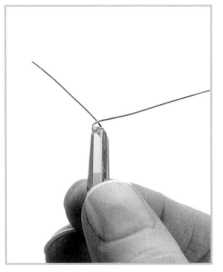

2 Insert 1 in. (2.5cm) of wire through a keystone. Bring both wires to the keystone's center top, and cross them. Wrap the short wire around the long wire to make a $^3/_{32}$-in.-long (2.4mm) collar. Cut off any excess short wire. Use chain-nose pliers to press the end flush against the wire.

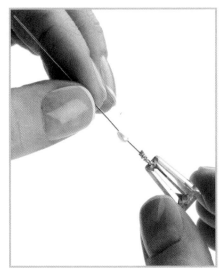

3 Thread one pearl onto the long wire, sliding it down to the collar.

6 Use chain-nose pliers to grip the headpin at the crimp bead; then make a bend in the pin at a 90-deg. angle.

Caution

It is exceedingly easy to crack the cubic-zirconium crystal. To lessen the risk, consider using tools (instead of your fingers) to make the wire-wrapped collar. After you have carefully crossed the wires (as shown), use the tips of bent-nose pliers to hold the wires where they cross, and use chain-nose pliers to wind the wire around the stem to make the collar.

7 Use round-nose pliers to grasp the headpin $^1/_8$ in. (3mm) from the bend made in step 6. Bend the headpin 180 deg. in the opposite direction.

4 Use the very tips of the round-nose pliers to make a wrapped loop ⅛ in. (3mm) above the pearl, stopping the wire wraps just short of the pearl. (See page 164, "Making a Wire Loop" for more details.) Repeat steps 2–4 with the second wire. Set both bead units aside.

5 Thread one bicone, one disk, and one crimp bead onto a headpin. Use crimping pliers to secure the crimp bead, making sure that the crimp bead, disk, and bicone bead are flush against the end of the headpin. If necessary, secure the crimp bead further with a drop of glue.

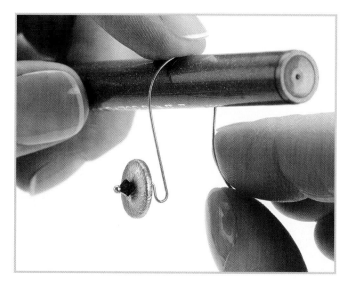

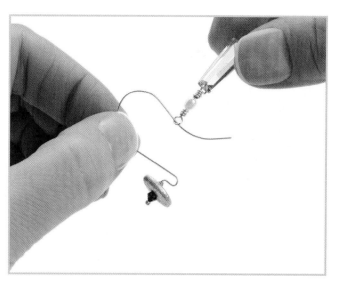

8 Mark a point ¾ in. (19mm) from the bottom loop on the headpin wire. Hold the marked point against the barrel of the marker with one hand, and bend the wire over the marker with the other hand. Take the wire off of the marker. Bend a curve at the wire's cut end so that it flares away from the earring. Trim the headpin end if necessary. Use a needle file and emery paper to deburr and smooth the end. Remove the mark with alcohol.

9 Thread a bead group set aside in step 4 onto the ear wire so that the flat side of the crystal faces forward and it sits in the loop below the disk. Repeat steps 5–9 for the second earring.

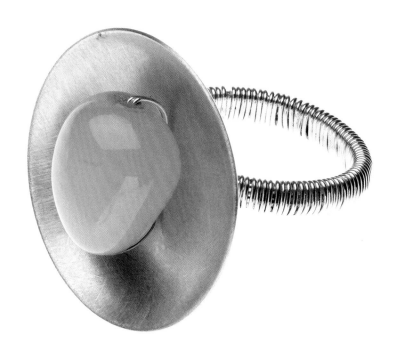

combine simple elements
for a design **with modern lines**
and retro spirit

Full Moon

The satiny, brushed surface of the shallow silver disk focuses beams

of reflected light through the center stone, bringing it luminously to life. Translucent beads, such as the glass celadon bead used here, or others, such as moonstone and rose quartz, acquire a mysterious inner glow when backed with a reflecting "mirror." A pearl's luster will be heightened from all sides, and it will seem to float, while cut transparent stones and faceted crystals appear to catch fire with brilliant sparkling rays.

MATERIALS

- 1 disk, sterling-silver, dome-shaped, 17mm dia. x 1.5mm thick
- 1 oval glass bead, celadon, 13mm wide x 15mm long x 9mm thick
- Wire, sterling-silver, 18-gauge
- Wire, sterling-silver, 24-gauge
- Scrap wire, 24- to 28-gauge

TOOLS

- Emery cloth, 200-grit and 600-grit
- Block of soft wood (such as pine)
- Hammer
- 1 common nail, 1¼" long
- Bead reamer with conical tip
- Needle file
- Ruler
- Wire cutters
- Chain-nose pliers
- Small bowl
- Ring sizing tool (see "Helpful Tip" on page 123.)

Making a Full Moon Ring

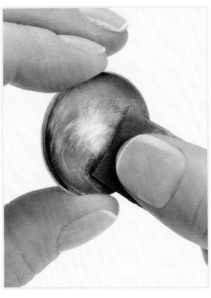

1 Pour some water into the bowl, and wet the 200-grit emery cloth. Use the wet cloth to smooth the edge of the disk.

2 Wet the 600-grit emery cloth. Use the cloth to rub the inside of the disk to a matte finish.

3 Place the disk, concave side up, on the block of wood. Use a hammer and nail to drive a tiny hole through the center of the disk.

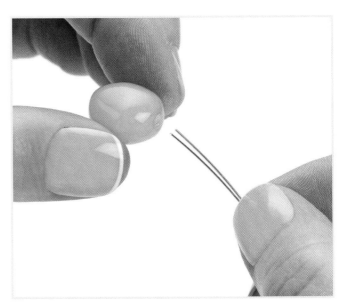

5 Use wire cutters to cut a 10-in. (25.4cm) length and a 48-in. (121.9cm) length of 24-gauge wire.

6 Holding both wires together, insert them through the hole in the oval bead. Slide the bead along the wires to the center of the 10-in. (25.4cm) wire. Have the 48-in. (121.9cm) wire extend 8 in. (20.3cm) from one side of the bead.

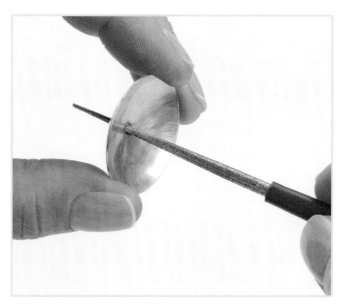

4 Use a bead reamer followed by a needle file to smooth the rough edges around the hole, making sure that the hole measures approximately $^1/_{16}$ in. (1.5mm) in diameter.

•••helpful tip•••

*Slip a ring that fits
you onto a dowel, a marker,
or other cylindrical object that has
a slightly smaller diameter than
your ring finger. Use this
as your ring-sizing tool.*

7 Bend the wires around the sides of the bead.

8 Continue to bend the wires around to the center under-side of the bead so that they meet. Use chain-nose pliers to bend the wires straight down.

Making a Full Moon Ring

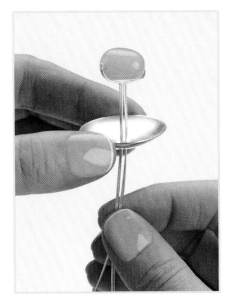

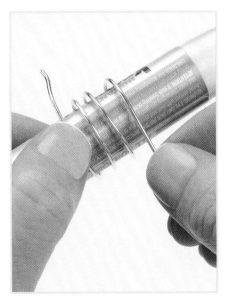

9 Thread the wires through the disk hole. Make two pairs, grouping a 5-in. (12.7cm) length and the 8-in. (20.3cm) length, and the other 5-in. (12.7cm) length and the 40-in. (1.0m) length.

10 On the underside of the disk, use chain-nose pliers to bend one of the wire pairs to the right and the other pair to the left, leaving a $^{1}/_{16}$ -in. (1.5mm) space under the disk.

11 To make a ring core, use wire cutters to cut an 11-in. (27.9cm) length of 18-gauge wire. Wrap the wire four times around the ring-sizing tool. (See "Helpful Tip" on page 123.)

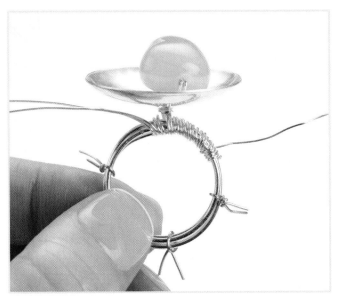

15 To secure the disk to the ring core, wrap one pair of wires a few times around the ring core under the disk. Repeat with the second pair of wires, wrapping in the opposite direction.

16 Move the 8-in. (20.3cm) length of wire aside. Starting under the disk, wrap each short wire around the ring core on each side of the ring. Remove the scrap wire as needed. Use chain-nose pliers to press the cut ends of the wire flush against the core.

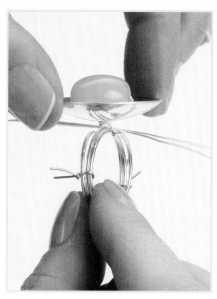

12 Adjust the coils of wire to your finger size. Make the fit loose to allow for the wire wraps. Use wire cutters to trim the ends so that they begin and end at the same point.

13 Push the coils together, and position them so that the cut ends are at twelve o'clock. Use lengths of scrap wire to secure the coils together at three, six, and nine o'clock.

14 Position the disk over the cut ends of the ring core at twelve o'clock. Have the wires perpendicular to the ring core.

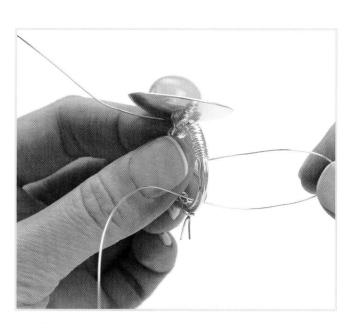

17 Wrap the 40-in. (121.9cm) wire around the ring core, beginning and ending under the disk. Remove the scrap wire as you wrap the wire. Use wire cutters to trim the end to $1/16$ in. (1.5mm). Tuck the end under the disk.

18 Make a stabilizing collar by wrapping the 8-in. (20.3cm) length of wire around the four wires connecting the disk to the ring core. Wrap the wire from the ring to the disk until the disk does not wobble. Use wire cutters to trim the end. Use chain-nose pliers to press the cut end flush against the wire under the disk.

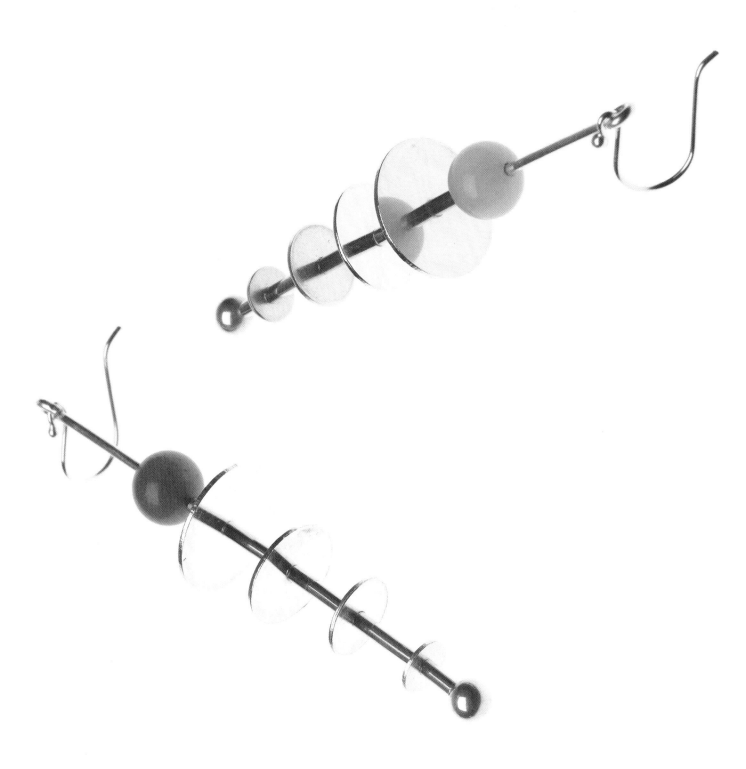

disks **and tubes combine for** modern "Jane Jetson" **style**

Retro Moderne

There is a wide range of stringing parts and jewelry components, such

as end caps and spacers, that are interesting in their own right, and using them in creative ways can produce novel results. In these earrings, finely made sterling-silver spacer disks and tubes, usually used as separators, are threaded onto a thin core wire. Their small holes allow them to stay centered on the wire, giving the stacked findings the appearance of solid, soldered pieces crafted by a jeweler.

MATERIALS

- 2 spacer disks, sterling-silver, 16mm dia. x 1mm thick
- 2 spacer disks, sterling-silver, 13mm dia. x 1mm thick
- 2 spacer disks, sterling-silver, 10mm dia. x 1mm thick
- 2 spacer disks, sterling-silver, 7mm dia. x 1mm thick
- 6 tubes, sterling-silver, 10.3mm long x 2mm dia. x
- 4 tubes, sterling-silver, 4.8mm long x 2mm dia. x
- 2 round dyed-stone beads, 8mm dia.:
  1 pumpkin orange
  1 butterscotch yellow
- 2 half-drilled round end beads, sterling-silver, 5mm dia.
- Wire, sterling-silver or silver-plated, 16-gauge
- 1 pair fish-hook ear wires with ball-end, sterling-silver

TOOLS

- Ruler
- Wire cutters
- Cyanoacrylate gel (instant glue)
- Round-nose pliers
- Chain-nose pliers
- Bent-nose pliers
- Bead reamer (optional)

Making Retro Moderne Earrings

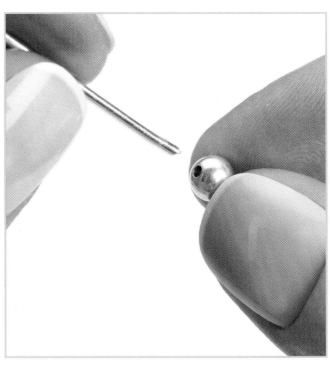

1 Use wire cutters to cut two 3-in. (7.6cm) lengths of wire. Make sure that both wires are straight by rolling them on a flat surface. Straighten out any bends using your fingers.

2 Apply glue to one end of each wire. Insert the wires into the end beads. Let the glue dry. Set one wire assembly aside.

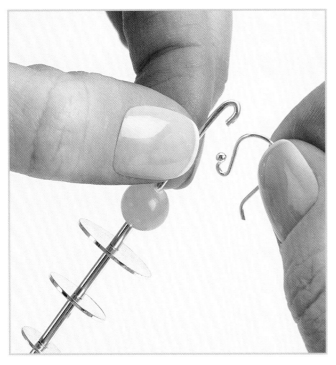

5 Thread on an ear wire.

Customizing Findings

If you cannot find an item with exact specifications, it is possible, in some instances, to customize what is available. If you can't find spacer disks or end beads with holes in the correct diameters, buy them with holes that are too small. Use a bead reamer (a conical file with a needle-sharp point) to enlarge the holes: insert the tip of the file into the hole, and slowly roll the reamer between your fingers while gently applying pressure. This will grind away the metal and enlarge the hole. Test-fit the core wire in the finding's new hole to ensure the right diameter.

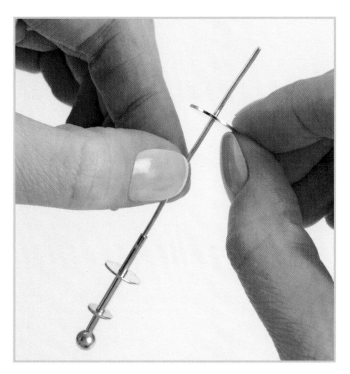

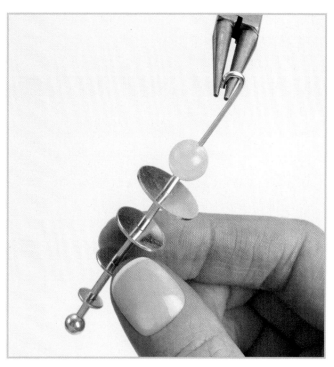

3 Thread the following onto the wire assembly: 4.8mm tube, 7mm disk, 10.3mm tube, 10mm disk, 10.3mm tube, 13mm disk, 10.3mm tube, 16mm disk, 4.8mm tube, and one stone bead.

4 Use the tip of the round-nose pliers to start making an eye loop at the top of the wire. Do not finish the loop.

6 Use round-nose pliers to finish the eye loop. Repeat steps 3–6 for the second earring.

●●●helpful tip●●●

The core wire must be straight if it is to pass through the small holes in the spacer disks and tubes. If you are using spool wire, straighten the length you need before cutting it. Grasp the spool in one hand, and stroke the loose end of wire with the fingers on your other hand; then cut the straight wire off the spool.

a dainty ring blooms with
nosegay of sweet flowers

Bouquet

Modern high-quality plastic flowers inspired by tiny vintage-glass

flowers are demure decorations that add sweet romance to handmade jewelry. Here, the flowers are combined to make a jeweled bouquet for a ring. In a palette of sunny tones—tangerine, pink, red, and lemon-yellow—the flowers are combined with a few green leaves to complete the illusion. Made in a few easy steps, the floral bouquet can be added to a barrette for a sweet touch of spring.

MATERIALS

- *2 frosted plastic leaves, 11mm wide x 19mm long:*
  - *1 pale green*
  - *1 lime green*
- *13 frosted plastic-flower beads, assort. colors, 10mm dia. x 7mm thick:*
  - *3 red*
  - *2 tangerine*
  - *2 pink*
  - *4 lemon yellow*
  - *2 clear frost*
- *13 spacer beads*, gold, 4mm dia. x 1mm thick (*daisy or Bali style with balls at edge)*
- *13 seed beads, opaque gold, size 11/0*
- *1 wire dome with loops, gold-plated, 16mm dia. x 9mm thick*
- *Transite*
- *Wire, gold-plated, 28-gauge*
- *1 faceted glass ring, red, size to fit x 6mm wide*

TOOLS

- *Ruler*
- *Wire cutters*
- *Beading needle, #10 (or long sewing needle with eye large enough for Transite to pass through)*
- *Cyanoacrylate (instant glue)*
- *Bent-nose tweezers (optional)*

Making a Bouquet Ring

1 Use wire cutters to cut an 18-in. (45.7cm) length of Transite. Thread the needle with the Transite.

2 Use a square knot to tie the Transite ends to the center of the top loop of the wire dome. Secure the knot with a drop of glue, and let it dry. Use wire cutters to trim the end close to the knot.

5 Repeat steps 3–4 to add additional flower groups, working around the center flower and down the dome to add the flowers in a staggered row, positioning the flowers so that no two of the same color are next to each other.

6 Add flower groups until the dome is covered, leaving room at one edge for the leaves. Make a double knot in the Transite. Do not cut it. Note: even a narrow space will work as the leaves can drape gracefully over the edge of the dome.

7 Insert the needle under the loop close to the edge of the dome. Thread two leaves onto the knotted Transite; then insert the needle under the same loop on the dome, and pull the Transite to tighten it and to seat the leaves. Remove the needle. Tie a square knot; apply a drop of glue; let it dry. Trim the excess Transite close to the knot.

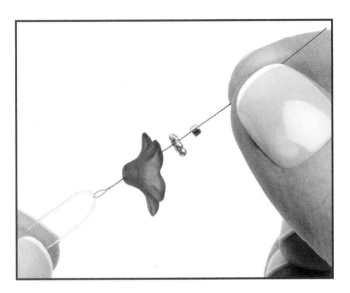

3 Thread one flower, one spacer bead, and one seed bead onto the needle.

4 Thread the needle back through the spacer bead, flower, and a loop of the dome that is near the knot (tied in step 2). Pull the Transite to tighten it and to seat the bead. Note: the flower group will be floppy.

8 Cut a 12-in. (30.5cm) length of wire. Thread one wire end over the crossed bars on the underside of the wire dome—keep the wire ends even. Wrap each end around the ring and over the crossed bars eight to twelve times, pulling the wires taut each time to secure the ring to the dome. Use tweezers if necessary. Trim away the excess wire.

variation

CHANGE TO SWEET COLOR

The bright fruity colors of the original "Bouquet" ring make the ring fun to wear in the spring and summer. For a ring that is more sweet and romantic, choose flower beads in a pastel colorway (right), such as strawberry, baby pink, and clear frost. Combine the flowers on a pink glass ring, and add crystal beads for sparkle instead of the green leaves to maintain the soft monochromatic theme.

BEADING BASICS

ALL THE TOOLS, MATERIALS, AND TECHNIQUES YOU'LL NEED

Basic Tools

The goal of this section is to help you set up a basic kit of beading essentials so that you can make every piece of jewelry in "The Collection," as well as those of your own design. You will probably want to add more enhancements to your kit as your interest in beading grows. In all cases, however, the number of essential tools needed to begin is surprisingly small. Although not shown, some household items such as cotton swabs and tape are also needed.

●●● Tools

Round-Nose Pliers
Essential for making smooth and round loops in wire, these pliers can be identified by their conical, tapered jaws.

Needle-Nose Pliers
Easily found in hardware stores, needle-nose pliers are readily available from jewelry suppliers and craft stores specializing in beading. They come in a wide range of sizes. Look for ones that fit comfortably in your hand, with tips that come to a narrow taper. Spring-loaded handles that stay open are very useful for beading as they allow for easier handling. The inside surface of the jaws should be smooth rather than serrated so that the pliers don't leave impressions on findings and wire. Some pliers will have a built-in wire cutter that is fine for emergency use, but these cutters generally produce unacceptably jagged cut ends in wire.

Crimp-Forming Tool
Used after a 2mm sterling-silver or gold-filled tubular crimp bead is secured to a .019-in. flex wire, this tool is designed to shape the bead into a neat, little ball. The pliers have a hollow globe-shaped mold embedded in its jaws in which the crimp bead tube is squeezed.

Chain-Nose Pliers
The jaws of this style pliers are smooth and flat, making them suited to grabbing small jewelry-making items that are within easy reach. The tips of these pliers are not long enough to access narrow recessed spaces.

GETTING STARTED

Here is an illustrated glossary of the essential tools you will need to make glamorous beaded jewelry. Some tools are indispensable to beading whether you are a beginner or veteran beader. Some tools are nice to have, making certain beading techniques slightly easier to do. Inexpensive tools may be adequate for occasional use, but when you begin to bead more seriously, you may decide to upgrade your tools to those that are of better quality.

Wire Cutters

Similar in appearance to a pair of pliers, wire cutters are actually pincers designed to cut wire with ease. If you have trouble cutting with them, try a pair with larger handles that will give you better leverage.

Spring Clamps

Clothes pins and alligator and binder clips can be used to keep beads from slipping off the end of strand material, but a spring clamp that has soft plastic pads is better for gripping beads without damaging them. Small 2- to 3-in. (5.1cm to 7.6cm) models work well.

Crimping Tool

Designed for squashing crimp beads and crimp tubes that secure strand material, this tool is easily found in craft stores. It has two indentations on its jaws; one flattens the crimp bead and the other folds it over tightly to produce a neat "stop" that keeps beads from sliding off the strand.

Thread-Cutting Scissors

A pair of sharp scissors in this style is much better than regular household scissors. Designed for making clean cuts in fiber strands, their perfectly aligned, fine steel blades make a much neater cut without causing fraying. Their characteristically sharp tip is also handy when trimming down a cord neatly to a nub.

Tools

Dowels

Round sticks are useful when bending or shaping wire. Whether a dowel or a toothpick, round sticks provide a uniform diameter for making loops and rings and do not yield when the jewelry-making wire is wound around them.

Adhesives

High-tack craft glue and permanent jewelry glues can add extra security to tied knots in silk cord or Transite line. Cyanoacrylate, also known as "instant" glue, can be used to attach bead caps to the end of memory wire. Instant glue, which is available in a "quick-set" variety, and beading glue provide strong, perma-nent bonds.

Tweezers

Tweezers make it easy to pick up tiny beads and to hold and twist loops in fine wire. Tweezers are available in different styles with ends that are straight, angled, or tapered.

Wooden Beads

Round beads made of wood are excellent spacer beads, especially when you are constructing a piece of jewelry comprising two parts that need to be kept apart. Wooden beads come in various diameters, so you can always find the size that you need. Softer than most beading materials, the wood will not scratch or mar surfaces.

Beading Needles

With thicker or stiffer strand material, a needle is not essential. But with thinner and harder-to-see material, such as Transite, beading needles can be very helpful. Essentially dou-bled-over and twisted pieces of very thin wire, beading "needles" can be made easily or can be purchased in inexpensive packs.

Wood Block

A block of wood can be used as a "stage" when using a hammer or awl to texturize and pierce metal findings. Hard enough to resist the pounding and soft enough not to scratch or mar the find-ings, a wood block also pro-tects your work surface.

Containers

Keeping beads organized is very helpful. Use lidded containers to keep beads together, or at the very least, use resealable clear storage bags (like sandwich bags in smaller sizes) to help group similar beads together.

Stackable Vials

As you become more serious about beading and you accumulate a collection of beads, consider upgrading your containers to stackable vials. These come in various sizes and are made in a variety of materials, such as clear plastic, glass, and aluminum with glass tops. Containers made in transparent materials allow you to scan your collection quickly for the desired beads.

Bead Dish

Suited to working with small beads, such as seed beads, a dish with a "shoulder" provides easy access to the holes in the beads. Stabilize lighter-weight dishes using clay adhesive.

OTHER OPTIONS FOR YOUR BEADING KIT

Molded Beading Tray Beads will roll if placed on a flat table. To avoid this, invest in a flocked beading tray that prevents beads from rolling and bouncing. The trays are designed with concentric, arc-shaped grooves, handy for composing the design of your strands before you start beading. The trays can be set aside in the middle of the project and set out again when you are ready to continue to bead.

Painter's Palette Available at art-supply stores, a painter's palette has shallow wells in which you can distribute your beads. There are heavier palettes made of ceramic that are more stable than the palettes made of pressed metal, although they are more expensive. Another option is to use disposable plastic palettes or cans with snap-on lids.

Needle-Threader A commonplace item, the needle-threader has a fine wire loop on the end of a plastic handle that opens up when it passes through the eye of the needle. Thread is inserted into the loop, and the loop is withdrawn from the eye of the needle, taking the thread with it.

Bench Clamp An inexpensive clamp that attaches to the edge of a table can be very handy as a "third hand" when you are carrying out a technique that requires both hands.

●●● Tools

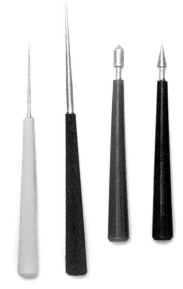

Bead Reamers

Slender diamond-tipped bead reamers are intended for use on glass, ceramic, or stone beads. The red- and yellow-handled reamers are suited to opening and enlarging bead holes. The green- and the blue-handled reamers are suited to smoothing the holes' rough edges, keeping the fibrous strand material from fraying as it passes through the holes. When using a reamer, apply slow, gentle pressure to avoid breaking or chipping the beads.

Wire Brushes

Brushes made from stainless steel or brass are suited to adding textural finishes to metal surfaces. Stiff steel bristles can abraid surfaces, producing patterns in the metal; whereas, softer brass bristles can add a glowing patina to some metals, such as sterling silver. The brushes are readily available in hardware stores.

Crochet Hook

Borrowed from needlework, the crochet hook is a handy tool that makes it easy to pull a cord through a knot or to get hold of a wire loop that is hard to reach.

Clamps

Small plastic clamps are easy to find in hardware stores. They are lightweight and suited to anchoring fine wire or other strand material. They are easy to manipulate as they are designed with a spring-loaded joint.

Nail Files

Cardboard and metal nail files are handy tools for smoothing or abraiding small metal surfaces. A cardboard emery file can be used to smooth the ends of metal wire or add texture to flat metal findings; however, it is prone to breaking and wearing out over time. The metal file works much like the cardboard nail file except it has an inflexible metal shaft and is a more durable a tool for smoothing and texturizing.

Claw hammer

A common household hammer can be used in some jewelry-making tasks, such as flattening or shaping metal findings or wire. To avoid marring the surface of the metal being worked on, wrap a layer of chamois cloth around the head of the hammer, using a rubber band to secure it. (If a textured surface is desired, do not cover the head of the hammer.) Place the item on a wood block and hammer it.

Emery Paper

Emery paper is dark gray in color and very finely textured; it is suited to refining and smoothing surfaces, including glass and metals. Coarse emery paper (200 grit) is often used in sequence with medium-grit (400 grit) and fine-grit (600 grit) papers. When emery papers are used with water, they produce an effect that is more satin in texture; when used dry, they produce a more coarse and scratchy finish. To smooth the ends of wire, lay the emery paper on a flat surface, and drag the rough wire end over the surface, rotating the wire until a smooth end is produced.

Emery File

Made to smooth down metal, the long narrow shaft of the emery file is suited to reaching metal in recessed areas or those items with narrow diameters, particularly the ends of cut wire, handmade jump rings, and squashed crimp beads.

Basic Materials

••• Beads

This illustrated glossary of bead styles is designed to help you identify the kinds of beads used in the making of the pieces of jewelry in "The Collection." While there is an infinite number of beads available to you, these few represent the basic categories of bead styles. They are grouped by their dominant characteristics such as shape or surface finish. Some beads fall naturally into two different groups.

Round

Round beads come in the classic ball shape. Their size is identified by diameter (dia.) which can range from 2mm (tiny) to 15mm (large). The holes in round beads are drilled through their centers. They are available in an infinite variety of materials, colors, opacities, and surface finishes.

Oblong and Oval

Oblong and oval beads are usually drilled through their long axis, although some are drilled through one end so they can be offset in a design. They are measured by length and by thickness. Dagger beads are typical beads in this style group.

Rondelle

Rondelle beads are round beads that are flattened along the drilled axis, like a summer squash. They can be faceted or smooth, and they are made in materials from plastic to crystal.

Nugget

Nugget beads refer to any irregularly cut stones. A tumbled nugget is treated to agitation that polishes its surfaces. Nuggets have an organic look, like they have been mined from the earth.

Faceted

Faceted beads have flat cuts across their surface that refract light, making them sparkle. They may be uniformly geometric in shape, or they may have irregular shapes with irregularly sized facets. Crystals fit into this group.

Briolettes

Briolettes are pear-shaped or teardrop-shaped beads that can be polished or faceted. Slightly plump in profile, they have head-drilled holes across their tips so they look like drops when they are strung on a strand.

Teardrops

A teardrop bead fits in the briolette group. Its name describes its shape. It can be distinguished from the pear-shaped briolette by its elongated silhouette. Made in plastic, glass, and precious stone, these beads are usually used as accent beads or pendants.

Bicone

Bicone means "two cones," which accurately describes the shape of these beads. Crystal bicones come in either a faceted or polished finish. Their holes are drilled along their axis.

Chips

Chips refer to any fragments of glass, stone, or other material that are irregular in size, often the result of breaking. Often polished until smooth, they have center-drilled holes.

Quartz

Quartz is a versatile mineral that is naturally snowy white, gray, or rose in color. Quartz is dyed to change its color and cut with facets to simulate semiprecious stones.

Pearls

Pearls are not just the classic round pearly-white, expensive gems they once were. Improved dyeing techniques now produce pearls in fun colors. Pearl varieties include freshwater pearls that are cultivated, producing interesting shapes. Silk thread is recommended for stringing pearls.

Seed Beads

Seed beads, also known as rocaille beads, come in an infinite variety of colors, finishes, and materials. They are commonly sold on hanks that comprise several beaded strands. Seed beads are measured by number—the higher the number, the smaller the bead.

Lustrous

Lustrous beads have a metallic sheen on their surface that makes them appear to glow. Made in stone, metal, glass, and quartz, lustrous stones complement beads that are faceted and sheer, like bicone crystals. Fire-polished beads are noted for their luster.

Crackled

Crackled glass beads have natural or manufactured fissures or striations in their interiors that catch light, adding sparkle and textural interest. Crackled beads are usually transparent or translucent to maximize the effect of light passing through the cracks.

Translucent

Translucent beads allow some light to pass through them, so they appear to have inner glow. They often appear milky or cloudy in pale colorways. Beads with translucence come in faceted and polished finishes, as well as in every shape imaginable.

Hole Styles

Holes in beads vary widely. Those that have holes in the middle are referred to as *center-drilled* (c) beads. *Side-drilled* (s) beads have holes drilled across their short axis. *Head-drilled* (h) beads are often oblong with holes at their narrow ends.

••• Strands

There are many different materials on which beads can be strung. While it is easy to generalize, it is important to understand how each strand material behaves so that you can choose the strand for your project. As a rule, it is best to string heavy beads on strands that are strong enough to support their weight without breaking. For lighter beads, strand material options broaden immeasurably.

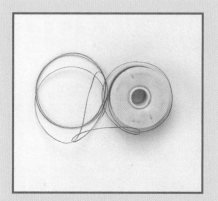

Silk Cord or Thread

Silk cord or thread is a strong natural material that is particularly suited to stringing pearls. Quite pliable, silk thread drapes well, but it must be knotted to be secured. Silk cord can fray, so condition it before stringing by pulling the thread through beeswax from the cut end toward the spool.

Plastic

A common plastic material used for beading is called Transite. A strand of Transite looks like transparent fishing line, and because it is nearly invisible, it is useful for stringing clear or pale-color beads. While quite strong, Transite is not as strong as Tigertail which has a reinforced metal core.

Braided

Braided wire is more flexible than ordinary wire and it is well suited to beading. Tigertail falls into this group; it has a braided stainless-steel core coated with clear plastic so it is smooth to the touch. Transite comes in varying thicknesses—the thicker being stronger. Be sure to test-fit the Transite to your beads for easy stringing. To secure your beaded strand, use crimp beads or tubes. (Knotting Transite is not recommended.) It is best to buy the same brand, matching the recommended sizes to achieve a sturdy closure.

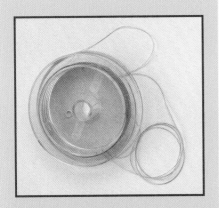

Elastic

Elastic line can be transparent and look like fishing line, but it's extremely "stretchy" and durable. It can be used for slip-on bracelets or for beads that would tear non-elastic strand material. It can be tied closed or crimped. It comes in a range of colors, making it appealing to beaders.

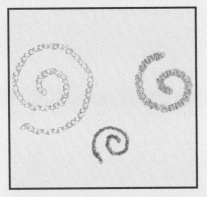

Chains

Chains are made by connecting links of wire together. They come in myriad link designs and finishes. They are used to support hanging decoration and to link parts of jewelry together. Sold by the inch, chains can be turned into jewelry by adding a clasp and beads on loops.

Wire

Wire is not used for stringing beads but rather to create findings such as loops and jump rings. It comes in different thicknesses called gauges. The larger the gauge, the thinner the diameter of the wire. In general the stiffness and strength of wire are determined by the metal used to make it.

Sterling Silver: Sterling-silver wire is made of silver that contains at least 92.5%, or 0.925 silver. The remaining percentage is copper. Silver is fairly soft but is easy to work with. It is easily polished to a high shine, and any scratches can be buffed out. Sterling silver is usually sold by weight, so if a thin gauge is used, it may not be too expensive to consider. Silver-plated wire can have a brass or copper core with the silver forming a thin layer on top. Some silver wire is tarnish resistant, having been treated by a chemical that retards oxidation.

Gold Plated: Gold-plated wire does not tarnish, making it an attractive choice for jewelry. The wire has a core of base metal such as copper and a thin layer of gold plating, making the wire reasonable in price. Pliers can scratch off the plated layer, so it is important to handle the wire with care. Brass wire appears gold in color, but it will tarnish over time.

Memory Wire: Memory wire is a special kind of wire that bounces back to its original shape after it has been pulled out of shape. It is available in various gauges and diameters. Suited to bracelets and necklaces, the wire does not require clasps to secure it. Instead, the very end of the wire can be bent flush against itself, or an end-cap bead can be secured with instant glue.

•••• Findings

Findings, ranging from the basic to the exotic, are the essential components that finish a piece of jewelry. Findings can help suspend beads or keep them apart. They can connect design elements, stop beads from sliding off a strand, and fasten jewelry together. Here are the essential findings you will need.

Headpins and Eye Pins

Headpins are short lengths of wire with either a ball, bar, or disk on one end. Eye pins have a hoop on one end. Both styles are threaded into bead holes and manipulated into loops using pliers. However, where head pins have a bead "stop," eye pins have an "eye" at the end through which another loop or pin can be threaded. Head and eye pins come in a variety of gauges and finishes.

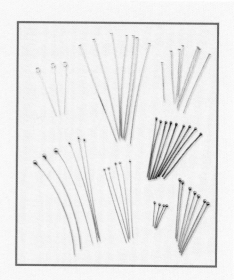

Jump Rings

Jump rings are very small metal hoops that connect jewelry-making components together. A jump ring might connect a beaded strand to a clasp, for example. Jump rings come in three styles: closed; open; and split. A closed jump ring has no split in it, so components must be secured using a knot or an open jump ring. An open jump ring has a split in the hoop so that loops or strands can be slipped on; the ring must be closed with two pairs of pliers. A split ring is a 1½-wind of stiff wire, much like a key ring, that must be forced open temporarily so looped beads can be slid on.

Spacer Beads

Spacer beads provide tiny spaces between beads so that the beads remain slightly separated and do not appear "squashed" together. Originally designed to be small and unobtrusive, spacer beads are now available with such interesting surface details that they become another design element with which to work when making jewelry. For example, daisy spacer beads have tiny balls around their edges, creating the look of a tiny flower.

Clasps

Clasps come in a wide variety of styles and finishes. Mechanical clasps are generally the most reliable for necklaces, including the lobster-claw shape, ring, threaded barrel, or sliding snap. S-hook, hook-and-ball, and toggle clasps are easier to work. Toggle clasps are especially suited to bracelets because they are easy to connect using one hand. Magnetic clasps are an attractive option for lightweight necklaces, but they are not secure enough for use on bracelets, which often get bumped around with normal wear.

Hanging Drops

Metal drops are used to provide added weight to a dangling bead, such as a pendant. They are available in a wide variety of shapes, sizes, and finishes. Used independently, they tend to draw the eye, adding design focus and interest.

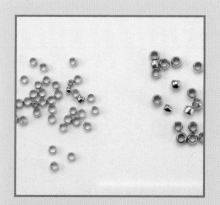

Crimp Fasteners

Crimp fasteners are small metal beads or tubes that are threaded on strands and squashed in place using a crimping pliers. The crimping process secures the end of a strand of beads so that the beads won't slide off. Crimping using crimp beads and tubes can also secure the end loop in strand material.

Earring Hooks

Earrings require a clasp to secure them to the ear. One popular style is the fishhook ear wire used for pierced ears. Available in a wide variety of metals, the crook section of the hook is threaded through the ear, and the little loop at the end of the crook is hung with beads or other decorative elements.

Buttons

While not usually associated with beading, buttons can be used in place of beads. Because they have holes or back loops, also called shanks, they can be strung on a strand or affixed to a loop as long as their decorative faces can be seen. Buttons are available in an infinite variety of diameters, materials, finishes, and styles.

Basic Techniques

●●● Stringing Beads

Almost any material that is safe to handle and has a hole through which a strand can be threaded can be a bead. While the process of beading is straightforward in principle, there are occasions when special tools or techniques may save you time and effort. Here are a few professional secrets to make your beading experiences more fun and successful.

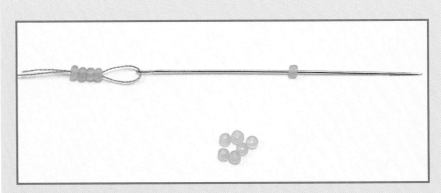

Using a Beading Needle

There are special beading needles that are thinner and longer than ordinary sewing needles. The appeal of using beading needles is that they allow many beads to be threaded on at a time, helping to avoid the cumbersome stringing of small beads that are often hard to handle. The eyes of beading needles are very small, so they are best suited to thin threads. For very tiny beads, use an embroidery needle with a blunt end. Pour the beads into a low, flat container, and guide the needle into the bead holes.

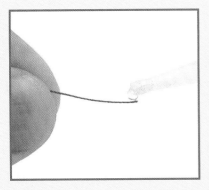

Using the Strand Material

Transform the thread on which small beads are strung into a "needle" by placing a ¼-in. (6mm) dab of cyanoacrylate (instant glue) at the end of the thread; let the glue cure; then use thread cutters to cut across the hardened glue to form a stiff tip. Refresh the end of the thread when necessary. Nail polish will also stiffen the thread, but it takes longer to dry.

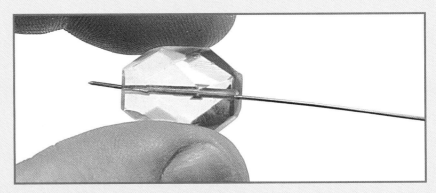

Using Your Fingers

Some strand material doesn't require any needle at all. If the strand material is fairly stiff, such as wire, Tigertail, or Transite, you can easily thread the end of the strand into the beads as long as the beads' holes are large enough. Oftentimes, the end of the strand frays or unravels, making it difficult to thread the material through the beads. In this case, apply glue or nail polish, as described in "Using the Strand Material" shown left, to remedy the problem as often as the strand material needs refreshing.

Making Your Own Beading "Needle"

It is easy to make your own "needle" to accommodate your beading needs.

1 Measure and cut a 6-in. (15.2cm) length of 28-gauge or stiff beading wire.

2 Fold the wire in half around a toothpick, as shown.

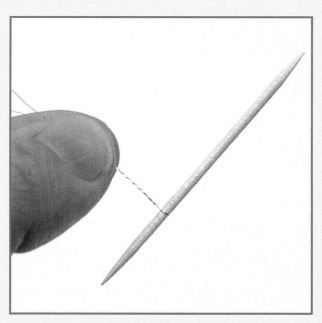

3 Twist the pair of wires between your fingers to form a straight spiral with a loop.

4 Slide the loop off the toothpick. Using wire cutters, snip the wires evenly across to make the "needle."

Using a Flexible Beading Needle

Another type of "needle" isn't really a needle at all. Flexible beading needles are actually very thin pieces of wire that are bent in half with a loop at one end. The loop is as large as $1/8$ in. (3mm) or more in diameter, so it can accommodate thicker strand

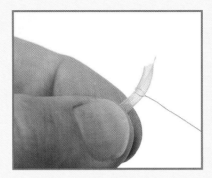

material, such as Transite; heavier braided silk cord; and even narrow widths of gauze ribbon. The large loop collapses as the strand material is pulled through the bead hole, so the needle is very versatile. They can be purchased, or made by hand. Refer to "Make Your Own Beading Needle," page 149.

Restringing Small Beads

Small beads, such as seed beads, will frequently come in packages, vials, or hanks. When the beads are "hanked," they are prestrung on single strands of cotton thread and knotted together at their ends. It is important to keep seed beads on the hank until you are ready to use them, but do not use the thread on which they came for your project. You will need to transfer the seed beads onto stronger strand material, as the cotton thread used to string them is unsuitable for use in jewelry making. The process of rethreading the beads can be very tedious. The following steps will make the job easier.

Measurements

BEAD SIZE

Bead size is usually indicated in millimeters. Generally, the higher the number, the larger the bead. Seed beads are an exception. Their size is indicated by numbers. The higher the number, the smaller the bead. A 5°, or E bead, is about 5mm wide; a 20° is slighter larger than a grain of sand.

Connecting Strand Materials

1 To string very tiny beads, glue the tip of the chosen strand material to the side of the thread that holds the beads, using instant glue.

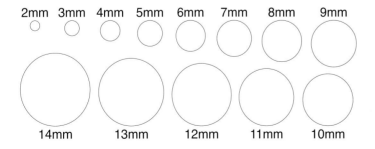

2mm 3mm 4mm 5mm 6mm 7mm 8mm 9mm

14mm 13mm 12mm 11mm 10mm

1 Lay the hank of beads on a flat surface. Identify the top knot or juncture where all the strands come together. Pick up one strand at the knot, and snip the thread using scissors. Carefully knot the end of the thread so the beads don't slip off.

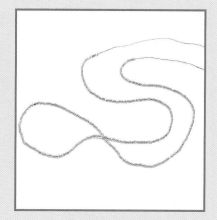

2 Find the opposite end of the same strand by following it back to the top knot. Hold the beads near the top knot, and snip the strand from the hank using scissors.

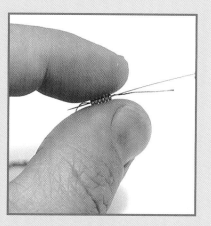

3 While holding the end of the beaded strand between your thumb and index finger, insert a beading needle through four to six beads. Slide the beads onto the needle, then onto the strand on the needle. Continue to transfer the beads to the new strand material as before.

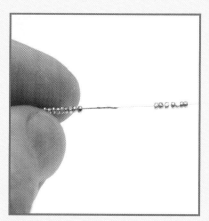

2 When the glue is dry, carefully slide seven beads over the glued section of strands to test the joint and to ensure that the remaining beads can pass over it.

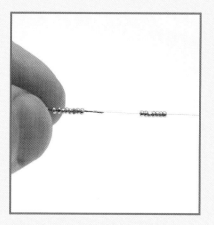

3 Continue transferring the beads from the original thread to the new strand material until the required number of beads are threaded on the new strand.

●●● design tip ●●●

Mix seed beads
in different finishes
such as glossy, transparent,
and opalescent to
create a design with
high style.

●●● Weaving Beads

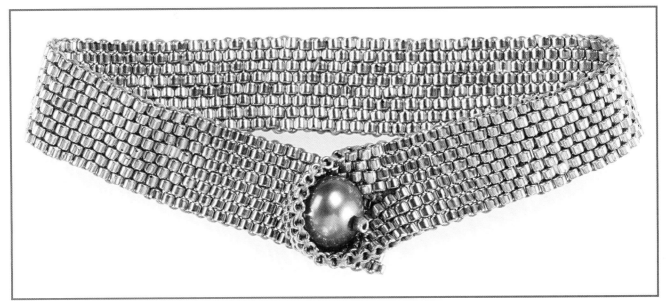

The "Liquid Gold" bracelet

PEYOTE BEADING

The "Liquid Gold" bracelet on page 18 and the "Infinity" pendant on page 84 are two designs that use flat even-count peyote beading. Although working the peyote-beading technique can be time consuming, the flat even-count weaving technique is easy to master, allowing even beginners to produce minimalistic designs that have elegant style.

GETTING STARTED

The success of peyote weaving depends upon all the beads being the same size and shape. There is a new type of precision-made seed bead that allows the tiny beads to lock together neatly in place. One brand to use is Delica seed beads. Although they are more expensive than traditional seed beads, they are satisfying to work with, producing near-perfect weaving results.

When you are ready to weave your beads, pour them into a large shallow bowl with a rim (or shoulder). If the bowl is light in weight, use an adhesive putty, such as Fun-Tak, to secure the bowl to the work surface. Some beads will gather at the edge of the shoulder and tilt up at a 45-degree angle; this will make the beads easier to prick up with the tip of a needle. Because peyote beading entails picking up one bead at a time, this small aid will help to prevent wrist strain.

Prestretching the thread

Beading thread may fray and stretch over time. It is recommended that the thread be prestretched prior to using it. This can be done easily by unfurling a length of thread from the spool and tugging at opposite ends to stretch it.

Conditioning the thread

Peyote beading goes faster and easier when the thread slides through the beads without tangling. Thread Heaven or beeswax can be used to condition your thread, but do not overcoat the thread or it will become sticky. Some threads, such as Nymo, work well without conditioning. Some threads, such as Silamide waxed nylon, are already conditioned.

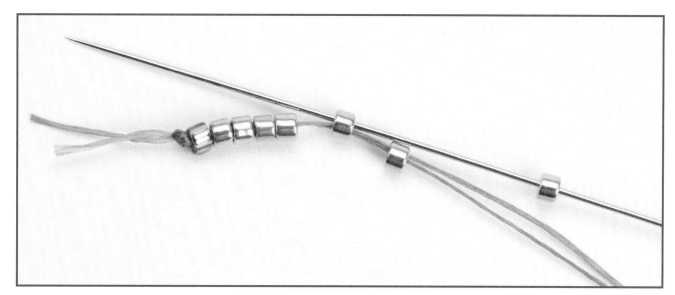

A six-bead width in a peyote weaving is a very manageable bead count, especially for a beginner.

TIPS FOR PEYOTE BEADING

Flat even-count peyote beading uses an even number of beads in each row. Count each row carefully to avoid having to undo a section.

The first few rows of the peyote weaving are the most diffi-

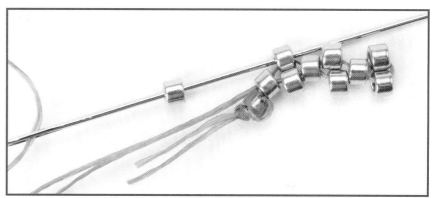

The first two or three rows are often unwieldly to work.

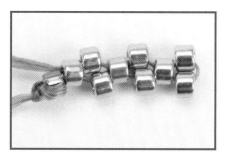

The weaving is beginning to take shape.

The weaving pattern is well established.

cult to bead because the rows don't line up easily. When working these rows, hold the work in your hands. However, once the peyote weaving is more established, do the weaving on a flat work surface. Hold the woven strip down, resting one fingertip on the leading row only when pulling the thread taut to seat the row of beads. Insert the needle on a diagonal. When you are inserting the needle through

a previously stitched bead, it should always slide through smoothly. Any friction may cause the thread to snag. If you feel resistance, pull out the needle, and reinsert it.

The quickest way to complete a row is to stitch in one direction. If you began on the right and worked to the left, turn the piece over when the row is completed so that the thread is on the right side. Then weave the next row from right to left again.

To ensure smooth and even rows, pull the thread taut after each row to remove any snags, loops, or slackness. If you have dropped a stitch or missed a bead, use the tip of the needle to loosen the thread at the beginning of the last row. Pull on the thread while gently guiding the needle, eye first, back through the beads until you can correct the mistake.

Attaching a new thread

Using extra-long thread makes weaving more difficult and allows the thread to tangle more easily. Because of this, most projects are made by either joining threads or joining beaded sections together. Here are two methods used to attach new threads when using seed beads with small and large holes.

■ **Small holes:** (Delica beads) When the thread is about 2½ in. (6.4cm) long, cut off the needle. Thread the needle with a new length of thread, making the ends even. Tie each end of the new thread to a tail of the old thread. Make a square knot in each close to the last bead. Apply glue to the knots; let them dry; and trim the ends, leaving tiny tails to push into the beads. Resume beading.

Slack threads produce an uneven weaving.

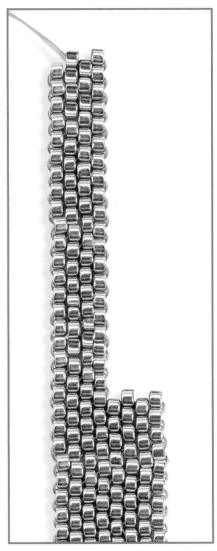

Taut threads produce an even weaving.

■ **Large holes:** (size 9/0 beads) When the thread is about 2½ in. (6.4cm) long, set the needle down. Thread another needle with a length of thread, making the ends even. Tie a knot in the ends. Apply glue to the knot; let it dry; and trim the ends. Insert the new needle through the beads along the same path the old thread took for the last

three or four beads. Tie a square knot to secure the new and old threads together. Apply glue to the knot; let it dry; and trim the ends. Insert one needle through the next few beads; then insert the other needle through the same beads, pulling the knot into the beads. Cut away the old thread, and resume beading with the new needle.

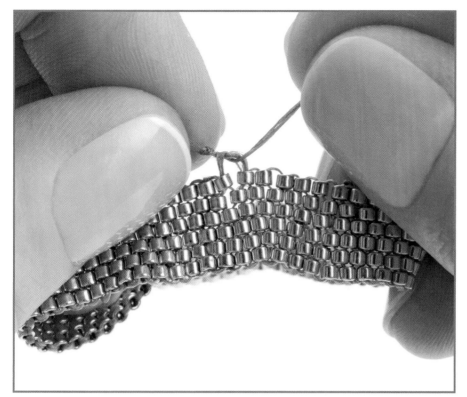

A neat square knot secures the rows at the oposite ends of a flat, even-count peyote weaving.

Attaching beaded sections

Bead a section. When the thread is about 4 in. (10.2cm) long, leave the threaded needle attached, and set the section aside. Bead a second section, leaving the threaded needle attached. Match the two sections. Use the needle from one section to weave through the last row of beads of the other section. At the end of the row, tie a square knot close to the beads; apply glue; let it dry; then trim the ends. Repeat with the other needle, weaving into the last row of beads of the other section.

Finishing your weaving

When you have finished your peyote weaving, wiggle it a bit to smooth out ripples and even up the edge stitches. Use a pin to undo the knot next to the stopper bead. Remove the stopper bead, and tie a square knot close to the first bead. Apply glue to the knot; let it dry; and trim the ends.

In the "Infinity" pendant, the woven strip is twisted and the opposite ends are stitched together.

Flat, Even-Count Peyote Weaving

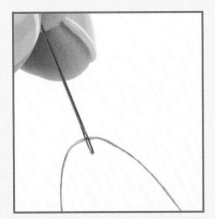

1 Thread a needle, and make the ends even. Tie a square knot in the ends using both strands. Note: the knot will be untied later, so don't pull it too tight.

2 Thread on a stopper bead. Note: to distinguish it, use a bead in a different color than any planned for your design.

3 Secure the stopper bead by inserting the needle back though the bead from the knot side and pulling it through.

7 To finish the row, thread on a bead (9). Skip the next bead from the previous row (2), and insert the needle through the following bead (1).

8 Pull the needle through, making sure that the threads are taut.

9 Turn the beaded section over so that the thread attached to the needle is on the right side. Start another row by threading on a bead (10). Insert the needle through the first raised bead from the previous row (9). Pull the threads taut.

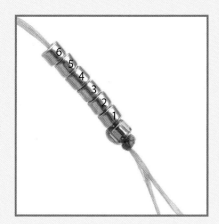

4 Thread on an even number of seed beads. Note: for the "Infinity" pendant, thread on six beads; for the "Liquid Gold" bracelet, thread on eight beads. Turn the strand over so that the stopper bead is on the opposite side.

5 Thread on a bead (7) to start the next row. Insert a needle through the second-to-last bead (5) in the previous row. Pull the needle through, making sure the threads are taut.

6 Thread on a bead (8). Skip the next bead from the previous row (4), and insert the needle through the following bead (3). Pull the needle through, making sure the threads are taut.

10 Thread on another bead (11). Insert the needle through the second raised bead from the previous row (8). Pull the threads taut.

11 Thread on another bead (12). Insert the needle through the third raised bead from the previous row (7). Pull the threads taut.

12 Repeat steps 9–11 to add another row. Continue to add rows until the band is the desired length. Cut the needle from the thread. Working close to the beads, tie the thread ends using a square knot. Apply a drop of glue; let it dry; and trim the thread. Use a needle to open the knot next to the stopper bead. Remove the bead. Tie the thread ends; then glue and trim them.

Crimping Strand Material

Crimp beads

Crimp tubes

Crimp-forming tool

CRIMP BEADS AND CRIMP TUBES

Crimp beads and crimp tubes are used to create strong and durable "stops" on strand material to keep strung beads from slipping off the strand. Each is a different shape, although both styles serve the same function. Crimp beads are round; crimp tubes are long. Made of metal, crimp beads and tubes come in varied finishes, such as silver, gold, and brass. They are made in different sizes, each suited to a different strand material. They are threaded onto a strand and squashed with a crimping tool. Crimping is faster and easier than hand knotting which is used for the same purpose, especially by beginners.

In general, crimp beads and tubes need to correlate to both the thickness of the strand material and the diameter of the hole in the bead being strung. The bigger the beads, the heavier or sturdier the cord must be—and the larger the crimp beads. If you are not sure which to choose, look on the back of the packaging. If you buy the same brand for both the strand material and the crimp bead, the package information will indicate the right choices, and you will be assured an effective crimp.

THE CRIMPING PROCESS

While the process of crimping a crimp bead and a crimp tube is the same, it is important to note that the crimping tool is used twice. First the crimp bead (or tube) is squashed into a crescent shape, and then the crimp bead (or tube) is folded over. The finished crimp bead looks like a small knot, and the finished crimp tube looks like a narrow rectangle. The distinction is important in the ultimate appearance of the piece of jewelry, so consider it beforehand.

Using a Crimp–Forming Tool

Position the sterling-silver crimped tube in the hollow in one jaw; squeeze the tool's jaws together. Repeat the process, repositioning the tube and squeezing the jaws together until the tube is a neat ball shape.

Using a Crimp Bead

1 Thread one end of the strand through the crimp bead, reinserting the end into the bead to form a loop.

PREVENTING BEADS FROM BINDING

A finished crimp is very unyielding when beads push against it. To prevent a strand of beads from binding and becoming inflexible, allow a small amount of space between the last bead strung and the crimp bead. For a standard 7-inch (17.8cm) bracelet, allow about ¹⁄₁₆ inch (1.6mm) between the last bead on the strand and the crimp bead. Instead of guessing, thread on a seed bead as a spacer; cover it with a tissue; and break it off the strand using pliers after you have attached the crimp bead. The missing seed bead will provide the needed ease.

A malformed crimp bead

FIXING A CRIMP BEAD

Occasionally a crimp bead will be malformed, off-center on the strand, or folded over sloppily. As a first remedy, try squeezing the crimp again with the tip of the crimping tool. If this doesn't work, do not over-work the bad crimp. This can both

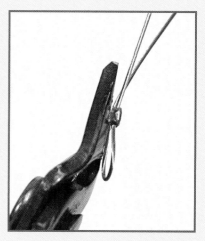

Wire cutters removing the crimp bead

weaken the metal and damage the strand material. Instead, begin again, removing the old crimp bead by carefully cutting along the side of the bead using wire snips or toenail clippers. Avoid cutting the strand material. The bad crimp bead will peel away easily.

2 Use the crescent-shaped space in the jaw of the crimping tool to squeeze the crimp bead.

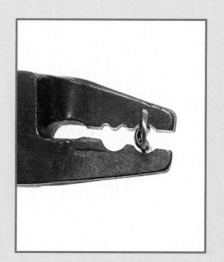

3 Use the round-shaped space in the jaw, clamping down on the crimp bead to trap the strand material.

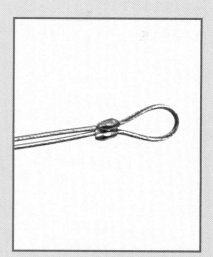

4 Check the finished crimp bead to make sure that it traps the strand. Note: the crimp bead will be round and compact.

Working with Wire

●●● Wire is a versatile material that provides sturdy and flexible connections between beads and on links and loops, depending on the chosen strand material. There are some basic guidelines for working with wire that will offer you consistently professional-looking results in your jewelry making. To begin, always wear eye protection when working with wire, as it can be unwieldy, and wire ends can go flying through the air when short ends are snipped. Put on safety goggles or glasses before you start work.

CUTTING WIRE

■ **Always use a pair of sharp wire cutters for the neatest cuts in wire.** Some needle-nose pliers have a wire-cutting slot near its pivot, and while it is suitable for occasional use, it is better to have a dedicated pair of wire cutters to produce superior cuts. Wire that is cut poorly can have undesirable bends, burrs, and snags.

■ **To cut wire of any kind, always cut straight across the wire.** Use the base of the pair of wire cutters rather than the tip for better leverage. Apply just enough firm pressure to make the cut. If the wire is not cut through cleanly, do not twist the pliers to force the cut, as this will only create sharp jags. Instead, release the pliers; reposition the jaws; and cut again. If this second effort doesn't work, it is possible that the blades of the wire cutter have become dull, so try to cut with a different part of the jaws. Sharpen or replace the wire cutter if these problems occur several times.

■ **Always wear eye protection when working with wire.** To cut heavy or stiff wire, use special caution because the wire may snap off when it is cut, sending a sharp piece flying. This is especially common when a short end of wire is cut. Be sure to wear eye protection to prevent injury. An easy way to keep short pieces from getting away is to carefully hold the end of the wire between your fingers while cutting the wire with the other hand. For longer lengths, hold the end with your hand, allowing the piece to drop in your hand when the wire is cut.

■ **Save your wire scraps, even the short pieces that are snipped off.** Some of the designs in this book may call for more wire in the materials list than is actually used. This is to make some allowance for the variations in the crafter's technique and to accommodate the need for an extra tail of wire for leverage when bending wire. Save any excess wire, especially sterling silver and gold plated, because it can be used to make jump rings, for example, for another project.

■ **Smooth the jagged or rough ends of wire.** While thin wire measuring more than 22 or 24 gauge will generally require little or no smoothing, thicker wires, such as those measuring 20 gauge, may have sharp edges that require it. Use emery paper to remove burrs from wire. Emery paper has a mixture of powdered emery (a mineral also called iron spinel) and glue that coats the paper; it also is available as emery cloth, where the fine abrasive coats a fabric. Emery sticks are also available where the abrasive paper is glued to a wood handle. The best emery papers are 200- and 400-grit. Remember that the larger the number, the finer the grain of abrasive surface. When using emery paper to smooth the jagged end of a wire: lay the emery paper on a flat surface, abrasive side up; drag the end of the wire gently across the surface of the paper at a 45-degree angle, rotating the wire to smooth the end evenly.

AVOIDING BREAKS

Metal wire must not be overworked by bending it back and forth. This weakens the metal, and the wire may eventually break. If a kink forms in the wire with which you are working, follow the recommendations below to fix the problem. If the kink cannot be fixed, restart with a fresh piece of wire.

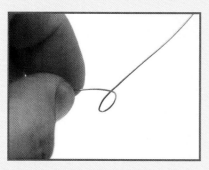

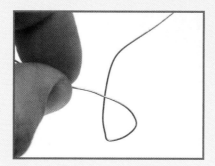

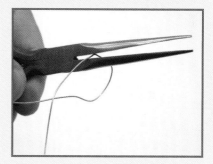

THE HISTORY OF A KINK

■ **A small kink often begins** as a small unwanted loop in the wire, an event common to wire crochet when a long tail of wire is pulled through a loop or wrapped around a bead.

■ **Don't pull the wire** in order to straighten the kink. That will only tighten it. Instead, use your fingers to open the loop of wire into a wide arc; then rotate the wire into a straight line.

■ **If a kink has formed,** flatten the section by gently squeezing it with the broad part of a pair of chain- or needle-nose pliers. Repeat, if necessary.

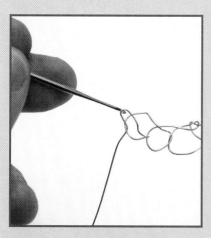

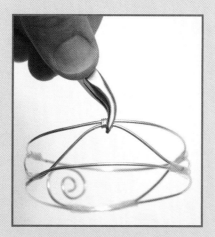

MANIPULATING THIN WIRE:

■ **Thin wire can be pulled** through narrow areas using a small crochet hook. To avoid damaging the wire and the hook, gently tug on the loop of wire, working it through slowly until the wire can be reached with your fingers.

■ **Bent-nose pliers can also be very helpful** in finishing a winding of wire when a pair of ordinary needle-nose pliers can't reach the wire or when extra leverage is needed. Avoid scratching the wire by pinching it carefully with the tip of the pliers.

●●● design tip ●●●

Wire can play a strong role in the design of your jewelry. Use wire with a unique feature, such as a square shape.

Successful Wire Wrapping

To avoid sloppy wire-wrapping, take your time and follow these few tips:

- ■ Keep the wire taut at all times
- ■ Wind only a few wraps at a time
- ■ Check your work as you go
- ■ Avoid kinking the wire

Cautions:

Do not attempt the same winding technique with a thin wire as you would with a thick wire. Pulling a thin wire back toward the hand holding both wires will only cause the thin wire wraps to pile on top of each other. Do not wind thick wire without checking every few winds for gaps because they can't be eliminated with the chain-nose pliers in the same way you can with the thin wire. The best way to wrap thick wire is to not have any gaps in the first place.

Thin Wire (Featured in "Water Lily" on page 90) When you are wire-wrapping with fine-gauge wire, follow these steps:

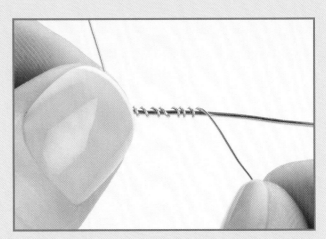

1 Position the thin wire against the base wire, leaving a 1-in. (2.5cm) tail. Hold both wires with one hand. Begin wrapping with the other hand.

2 Wrap the wire a few times. Do not be overly concerned with gaps between the winds.

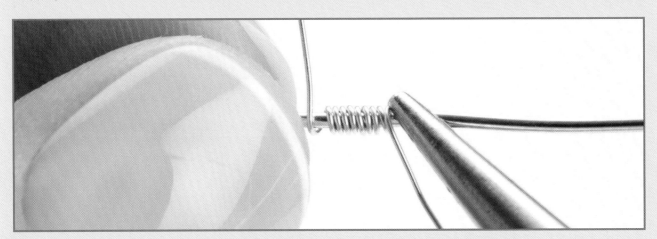

3 Use chain-nose pliers to slide the entire group of wrapped wires back toward the starting point to close all the gaps. Continue to wrap, repeating these steps as necessary.

Thick Wire (Featured in "Willow Branch" on page 30) When you are wire-wrapping with heavy-gauge wire, follow these steps:

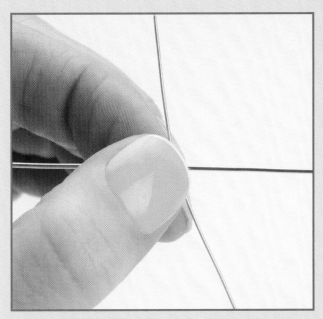

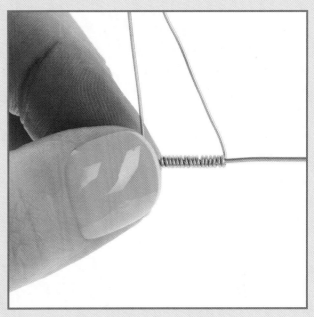

1 Position the thick wire against the base wire leaving a 1-in. (2.5cm) tail. Hold both wires with one hand. Begin wrapping with the opposite hand.

2 Wrap the wire a few times, but with each wrap pull the wire back toward the hand holding both wires.

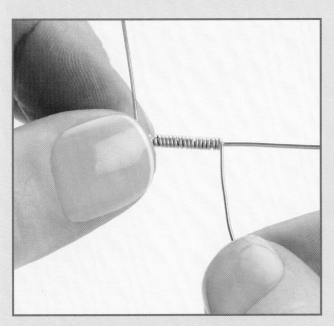

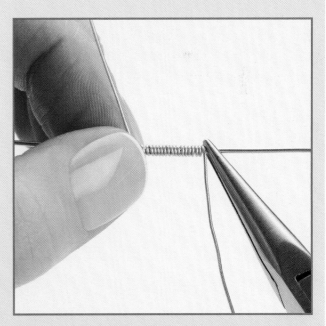

3 Continue to wrap the wire, pulling it back each time. This will help the last wrap tighten against the ones before, preventing gaps.

4 Check every few winds for gaps. Use chain-nose pliers to close small gaps by sliding the group of wrapped wires toward the starting point.

••• Making A Wire Loop

Making a wire loop using plain wire or a headpin is an essential technique when creating pendant beads or swiveling connections between parts of a piece of jewelry.

A loop is composed of two parts: the round loop and the wrapped stem. You will need a pair of round-nose pliers to make the round loops. You will also need a pair of needle-nose or bent-nose pliers to crimp the wire tail onto a wrapped stem. A pair of bent-nose pliers is highly recommended because the offset tip provides extra leverage when the wires are wound tightly into place, as is done when you are finishing the wrapped-wire collar.

Loops can be made in fairly large diameters (7 to 10mm), depending on the gauge of the wire used. In general, a thicker-gauge wire is suitable for large loops, and thinner-gauge wire is better for small loops (2 to 4mm). When making any loop, consider the size and scale of the bead.

Making the Basic Wire Loop

1 Choose a headpin whose length is at least 1 in. (2.5cm) longer than the bead. Thread the plain end of the headpin into the bead hole, allowing the bead to slide down to the head.

2 Use round-nose pliers to firmly grip the wire stem ³⁄₁₆ in. (4.8mm) above the bead. Rotate the pliers 45 deg. in one direction to form a bend in the wire stem.

5 Remove the loop from the pliers. Use the widest part of the needle-nose pliers to grip the flat face of the loop to straighten it. Note: to avoid scratching the surface, be careful not to slide the pliers across the wire.

6 Continue to push the wire around the stem of the loop, using your fingers to form a collar, making sure the windings are close together. Note: bent-nose pliers can also be used to wrap the wire.

A

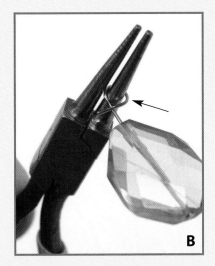

B

3 For a small loop, use the tips of round-nose pliers to grip the wire to make the loop. Note: the position on the pliers determines the diameter of the loop.

For a large loop, grip the wire near the bottom of the jaws of the round-nose pliers to make the loop. Note: the base of the pliers produces the largest loop.

4 Push the wire stem around the pliers using your fingertip, crossing in front of the bend in the wire.

●●●helpful tip●●●

Finishing the ends of cut wire is important. Smooth out rough cuts using an emery file, emery paper, or emery cloth.

7 Using wire cutters, snip off the excess wire when the windings are about two turns away from the bead. Smooth the wire end with an emery file.

8 Use bent-nose pliers to gently squeeze the wrapped-wire collar. Note: use caution to avoid cracking the bead.

Making a Wrapped Loop

There is a special case in jewelry making when a wrapped loop is preferable to—and more attractive than—the basic loop, and that is when you are making a loop for a bead with a head-drilled hole, such as a briolette. Instead of winding the wire around the stem only, as in a regular loop, you wrap the wire around the tip of the bead so that the wraps conceal the bead hole and provide an appealing decorative collar. Note: it is a good idea to first practice the wrapped-loop technique on a less-expensive bead.

1 Cut a 2-in. (5.1cm) length of 26-gauge wire. Thread it through the hole in the bead, leaving a ³/₄-in. (19mm) tail. Bend up both wires toward the top of the bead. Note: one wire will be shorter than the other.

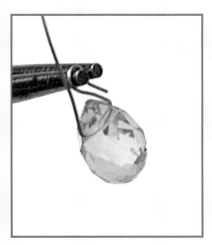

2 Grip the short wire using the round-nose pliers, and rotate the pliers to make a loop directly over the tip of the bead. Push the loop against the bead to make an "S" shape.

Making a Wrapped Loop with a Stem (Featured in "Willow Branch" on page 30.)

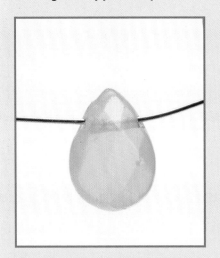

1 Thread the wire through the hole in the briolette. Bring the bead to the midpoint of the wire.

2 Bring both ends of the wire to the top of the bead, and cross them.

3 Use chain-nose pliers to bend one wire so that it is straight up and centered on top of the bead. Note: this is the wire stem.

3 Hold the loop with the needle-nose pliers, and use your fingers to bring the long wire around the back of the bead, past the "S" loop, and around to the front of the bead.

4 Continue to wind the long wire around the wire stem and the bead, moving downward, to conceal the hole in the bead and to complete the collar. Cut off any excess wire.

5 Use the tips of the needle-nose pliers to gently squeeze the wire collar, being careful not to squeeze so hard as to break off the tip of the bead.

4 While holding the wire stem in one hand, use your other hand to grasp the second wire, and begin to wrap it around the stem.

5 Continue wrapping the wire, working from the top of the bead down toward the bead hole to create a wire-wrapped collar.

6 Cut away any excess wire. Use chain-nose or bent-nose pliers to gently squeeze the wire end against the bead.

Making a Double Loop

There are times in jewelry making when you want to add a beaded link to a chain or you want to connect the parts of a dangling earring in a decorative way. In these cases, a double-loop (or two-loop connection) can be used. First, choose a loop wire that is similar, if not identical, to the wire used in the chain. If the chain is sterling silver, use silver wire; if the chain is gold-plated, use gold plated wire. Matching the loops to the chain gives the original piece a professional finish.

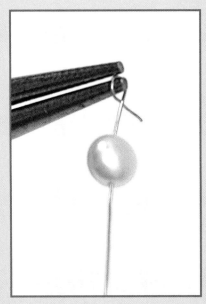

1 Thread a 2-in. (5.1cm) length of 24-gauge wire through a pearl, centering it on the wire. Use round-nose pliers to make a 4mm loop, ⅛ in. (3mm) from the pearl.

2 Repeat step 1 to make a 4mm loop, ⅛ in. (3mm) from the pearl on the opposite side of the pearl.

3 Use the tips of wire snips to cut off the excess wire at each loop. Smooth the ends of the wire using an emery file. Use needle- or bent-nose pliers to crimp the wrapped wire.

4 Snip out one link in the chain. Thread one end of an open jump ring through a loop on the pearl and a link in the chain. Close the ring.

5 Thread one end of a second open jump ring through the second loop on the pearl and the end link in the chain cut in step 4. Close the jump ring to connect the pearl to the chain.

Working with Jump Rings

OPEN JUMP RINGS

Open jump rings are particularly useful for joining components that have continuous loops that cannot be opened. The open jump ring is a simple hoop of metal with an open joint suitable to threading on looped beads. Jump rings need to be attached with care to ensure a secure closure, especially with wire that can slip between the joint or for heavy beads that can pull the jump ring out of shape, forcing it open.

••• helpful tip •••

Avoid pulling the ends of the ring apart sideways, as this can cause the jump ring to become distorted, making it difficult to match up its ends for a secure closure.

•

Avoid opening the jump ring any more than necessary because excess flexing can weaken the metal.

Attaching an Open Jump Ring

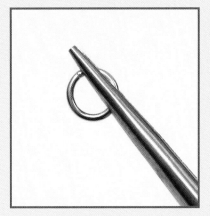

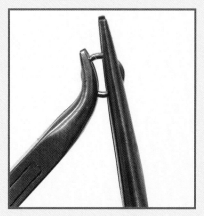

1 To create a connection using a jump ring, carefully open the ring by gripping it on one side of the opening with the flat part of a pair of needle- or chain-nose pliers.

2 Grip the other half of the opening using a pair of bent-nose pliers.

(Continued on page 170.)

Making Jump Rings

Making your own jump rings is easy. Although ready-made jump rings are inexpensive, you may not be able to find a jump ring that is the right size or in the right wire thickness or finish. If you already have stiff wire that matches your project, you can use it to make jump rings for your project.

1 Find a rod-shaped item, such as a toothpick, knitting needle, dowel, or any other item whose diameter equals the inside diameter of the ring you want to make. Note: the diameter of the rod will determine the diameter of the jump ring.

(Continued on page 170.)

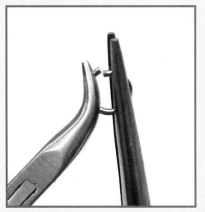

3 Carefully rotate the pair of bent-nose pliers toward you, pushing the needle-nose pliers away from you to move the ends of the ring out of plane.

4 Keep the jump ring clamped in the needle-nose pliers, and slip on the strand. Close the jump ring by bringing the ends of the ring together using the needle-nose and the bent-nose pliers.

5 Check to see that the closed jump ring does not have a gap between the ends of wire. If it does, use bent-nose pliers to squeeze the ring across its diameter and force the ends closed. Use caution to avoid distorting the shape of the ring.

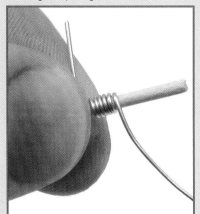

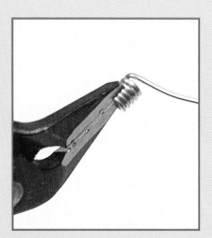

2 Hold the tail of a 4-in. (10.2cm) length of wire against the rod, and wind the length around the rod as many times as the number of rings you need. Note: even though a single jump ring requires only one wind of the wire, wind the wire two to three times around the toothpick to ensure that you make a complete jump ring.

3 Carefully slide the toothpick out of the windings of wire to reveal a coil. Use the very tip of a pair of sharp wire cutters to cut through the wire coil along one side. Note: this will cut the coil into individual split rings. If the wire ends are ragged, use emery cloth to smooth them.

4 Check to make sure the jump rings resemble little hoops with a split (or opening). Note: the split allows the ring to be opened and threaded through other loops or rings. Because the rings are so small, store them in a container with a transparent lid.

Working Index of Techniques

PLEASE REFER TO "BEADING BASICS" FOR THE FOLLOWING:

- Attaching Beaded Sections, 155
- Attaching a New Thread, 154
- Avoiding Breaks (in Wire), 161
- Crimping Strand Material, 158
- Finishing Your Weaving, 155
- Making a Double Loop, 168
- Making a Wire Loop, 164
- Making a Wrapped Loop, 166
- Making a Wrapped Loop with a Stem, 166
- Making Jump Rings, 170
- Stringing Beads, 148
- Tips for Peyote Beading, 153
- Weaving Beads, 152
- Weaving Flat, Even-Count Peyote Weaving, 156
- Working with Jump Rings, 169
- Working with Wire, 160
- Successful Wire Wrapping, 162

PLEASE REFER BACK TO THE PROJECT PAGES FOR THE FOLLOWING:

- Attaching a Button to a Weaving (Liquid Gold, 18)
- Attaching a Crimp-Bead Cover (Venetian Swirl, 60)
- Attaching a Disk to a Ring (Full Moon, 120)
- Attaching Monofilament to Memory Wire (Starburst, 26)
- Attaching Warped Findings to Wire (Waterlily, 90)
- Bending and Wrapping Wire (Zigzag, 112)
- Converting a Brooch to a Pendant (Classic Acorns, 102)
- Creating a Ribbon Bow (Classic Acorns, 102)
- Crimping Beading Wire (Cascade, 64)
- Crocheting Wire (Pastel Cloud, 12)
- Gluing Microbeads (Starfish, 78)
- Making Beaded Flowers (Bouquet, 130)
- Making Beaded Fruit on Loops (Deco Harvest, 96)
- Making Ear Wires (Carribean Waters, 108)
- Making Jump Rings, 170
- Making a Wired Flower (Trefoil, 54)
- Stringing Beads on Wire (Floating Pearls, 36)

NECKLACE AND BRACELET LENGTHS

Necklaces

Choker: 16 in. (40.6cm)

Princess: 18–20 in. (40.5cm–50.8cm)

Matinee: 23–27 in. (58.4cm–68.6cm)

Opera: 35–37 in. (88.9cm–94.0cm)

Bracelets

Women's: 7 in. (17.8cm)

Men's: 9 in. (22.9cm)

Anklet: 10 in. (25.4cm)

CHART OF BEAD MEASUREMENTS IN MILLIMETERS

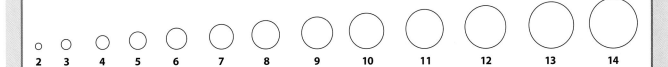

2　3　4　5　6　7　8　9　10　11　12　13　14

Use this chart to assess the approximate size of your beads. Place your bead within the circle above that is closest in size.

RESOURCES

Artbeads.com
11901 137th Ave. Ct. KPN
Unit 100
Gig Harbor, WA 98329
253-857-3433
www.artbeads.com
Beads and numerous findings

Bazaar Star Beadery
216 East Ridgewood Ave.
Ridgewood, NJ 07450
201-444-5144
www.bazaarstarbeadery.com
Loose and strung beads

Beads On Fifth Inc
376 Fifth Ave.
New York, NY 10001
212-244-6616 and 244-6615
www.beadson5th.com
Better-than-usual selection of
hardware in sterling and gold fill;
heavy on Swarovski crystals

Beads World Inc
1384 Broadway
New York, NY 10018
212-302-1199
www.beadsworldusa.com
Loose and strung beads

Blue Moon Beads
7855 Hayvenhurst Ave.
Van Nuys, CA 91406
800-377-6715
www.bluemoonbeads.com
Beads and findings

Earthstone Co.
112 Harvard Ave. #54
Claremont, CA 91711
800-747-8088
www.earthstone.com
Great online pictures of various
shapes and stones

Fire Mountain Gems and Beads
One Fire Mountain Way
Grants Pass, OR 97526
800-423-2319
www.firemountaingems.com
Beads and findings

Fun 2 Bead
1028 Sixth Ave.
New York, NY 10018
212-302-3488
www.fun2bead.com
Loose and strung beads, findings

Genuine Ten Ten
1010 Sixth Ave.
New York, NY 10018
212-221-1173
Loose and strung beads, findings

Honey Beads
P.O. Box 8309
Fleming Island, FL 32006
904-607-4699
www.honeybeads.com
Very wide selection of bead styles

LouLou Button
69 W. 38th St.
New York, NY 10018
212-398-5498
Gold buttons, findings, and chains

Margola Import Corp.
48 W. 37th St.
New York, NY 10018
212-695-1115
www.margola.com
Strung and loose beads, seed beads

Master Wire Sculptor, Inc.
1600 Clay St.
Vicksburg, MS 39183
www.wire-sculpture.com
Packed with materials and advice

Metalliferous
34 W. 46th St.
2nd Floor
New York, NY 10036
212-944-0909
www.metalliferous.com
Metal findings; wire; chain;
bangles; good source for tools

Michaels Stores, Inc.
8000 Bent Branch Dr.
Irving, TX 75063
800-642-4235
www.michaels.com
National chain of craft supplies,
including comprehensive beading
section with beads, tools, and wire

M & J Trimming
1008 Sixth Ave.
New York, NY 10018
800-965-9595
www.mjtrim.com
Ribbons and beads

New Age Enterprises
P.O. Box 14492
Tumwater, WA 98511
360-705-3299
www.gembeads.com
Not a wide selection but
has unusual items

New York Beads
1026 Sixth Ave.
New York, NY 10018
212-382-2994
Loose and strung beads

Tinsel Trading
47 W. 38th St.
New York, NY 10018
212-730-1030
www.tinseltrading.com
Cords and ribbons, trims,
buttons, and beads

Toho Shoji
990 Sixth Ave.
New York, NY 10018
212-868-7466
www.tohoshojiny.com
Beads, findings, and chains

Trim World USA
49 W. 37th St.
New York, NY 10018
212-391-1046
Strung and loose beads, and
gold and silver findings

Wonder Sources, Inc.
48 W. 38th St.
Ground Floor
New York, NY 10018
800-212-563-4990
www.wondersources.com
Loose and strung beads

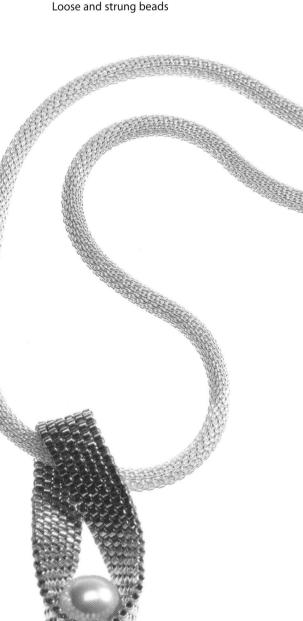

INDEX

Acorn cap, fit of, on bead, 105
Adhesives, 136
Agate for Quarry bracelet, 23, 24, 25
Aqua beads for Trefoil necklace, 55

Bakelite, colors of, 97
Bead dish, 137
Beading needle, 136
    making your own, 149
    stringing beads with, 148
    using flexible, 150
Bead reamer, 123, 138
Beads, 140–142
    restringing small, 150–151
    sizes of, 150, 171
    stringing, 148
Bench clamp, 137
Bent-nose pliers, 161
Bi-cones, 141
    for Floating Pearls necklace, 37
    for Les Anciennes earrings, 117, 119
    for Pastel Cloud bracelet, 13, 16
    for Starburst bracelet, 27
    for Trefoil necklace, 55, 57, 58
Bouquet (ring), 130–133
Bracelets
    lengths of, 171
    Liquid Gold, 18–21, 152
    Pastel Cloud, 12–17
    Quarry, 22–25
    Starburst, 26–29
Braided wire, 143
Briolettes, 141
    for Caribbean Waters earrings, 109
    for Cascade necklace, 65
    for Sunrise necklace, 45, 46, 49
    for Trefoil necklace, 55, 56, 57, 58, 59
    for Willow Branch necklace, 31, 34
Brooch, Classic Acorns, 103, 107
Buttons, 147

Caribbean Waters (earrings), 108–111
Carnelian nuggets for Sunrise necklace, 45, 49
Cascade (necklace), 64–69
Chains, 144
    ready-made, 87, 88
Chips, 141
Clamps, 138
Clasps, 146
Class Acorns (brooch), 103, 107
Classic Acorns (pendant), 102–107

Claw hammer, 139
Color saturation, 111
Containers, 137
Core wire, 129
Cracked glass beads, 142
Crimp beads, 158, 159
    for Cascade necklace, 66, 68, 69
    for Floating Pearls necklace, 38, 39
    Smart Beads versus, 111
    for Sunrise necklace, 48, 49
    for Venetian Swirl necklace, 61, 63
    for Willow Branch necklace, 31, 34
Crimp fasteners, 147
Crimp-forming tool, 134, 158
Crimping tool, 135
Crimp tubes, 158
Crocheted wire for Pastel Cloud bracelet, 13, 14
Crochet hook, 138
Crystal beads
    for Cascade necklace, 65
    for Water Lily pendant, 91, 94
Crystal nuggets for Caribbean Waters earrings, 109, 111
Cubic-zirconium crystals
    cracking of, as problem, 118
    for Les Anciennes earrings, 117

Deco Harvest (pendant), 96–101
Delica seed beeds, 152
    for Liquid Gold bracelet, 19
Double loop, making, 168
Dowels, 136

Earring hooks, 147
Earrings
    Caribben Waters, 108–111
    Les Anciennes, 116–119
    Retro Moderne, 126–129
    Zigzag, 112–115
Elastic line, 144
Emery file, 139
Emery paper, 139
End caps, 77
Eye pins, 145

Faceted beads, 141
Findings, 95, 145–147
    customizing, 128
Fingers, stringing beads with, 148
Flat-nose pliers, 134
Flexible beading needle, using, 150

Floating Pearls (necklace), 36–39
Full Moon (ring), 120–125

Garnets for Willow Branch necklace, 31
Glass beads
    for Floating Pearls necklace, 37
    for Full Moon ring, 121
    for Starfish pendant, 79
Glass flower beads
    for Deco Harvest pendant, 97, 98
    flattening, 98
    size of, 101
Gold-plated wire, 144

Hanging drops, 147
Head pins, 145
Hematite for Quarry bracelet, 23, 24
Hole styles, 142

Infinity (pendant), 84–89, 152

Jade beads for Quarry bracelet, 23, 24
Jump rings, 145
    making, 169–170
    open, 169
    attaching, 169–170

Kinks, 161

Lavender beads for Sunrise necklace, 49
Les Anciennes (earrings), 116–119
Liquid Gold (bracelet), 18–21, 152
Lustrous beads, 142

Magnetic-clasp loop for Water Lily pendant, 95
Memory wire, 144
Möbius, August Ferdinand, 85
Möbius strip, 85, 88
Molded beading tray, 137

Nail files, 139
Necklaces. *See also* Pendants
    Cascade, 64–69
    Floating Pearls, 36–39
    lengths of, 171
    Spring Peas, 70–73
    Sunrise, 44–49
    Teardrop, 40–43
    Trefoil, 54–59
    Trio, 50–53
    Venetian Swirl, 60–63

Willow Branch, 30–35
Needle-rose pliers, 134
Needle-threader, 137
Nugget beads, 140
Oblong beads, 140
Onyx for Trio necklace, 51
Oval beads, 140

Painter's palette, 137
Pastel Cloud (bracelet), 12–17
Pearls, 142
    for Cascade necklace, 65
    for Classic Acorns pendant, 103
    for Floating Pearls necklace, 37
    for Full Moon rforg, 121
    for Inffority pendant, 85, 89
    for Les Anciennes earrings, 117
    for Pastel Cloud bracelet, 13, 16
    for Starfish pendant, 79, 81, 82, 83
    varying sizes of, in related palate, 13
    for Water Lily pendant, 91
    for Zigzag earrings, 113, 115
Pendant bails, 52
Pendants. *See also* Necklaces
    Classic Acorns, 102–107
    Deco Harvest, 96–101
    Infinity, 84–89, 152
    Ruby Drop, 74–77
    Starfish, 78–83
    Water Lily, 90–95
Peyote beading, 152–157
    attaching beaded sections, 155
    attaching new thread, 154
    conditioning the threat, 152
    finishing, 155
    flat, even-count, 156–157
    for Liquid Gold bracelet, 19
    pre-stretching the thread, 152
    tips for, 153–155
Plastic-flower beads for Bouquet, 131, 132, 133

Quartz beads, 141
    for Classic Acorns pendant, 103
Quartz nuggets
    for Cascade necklace, 65
    for Ruby Drop pendant, 75

Resources, 172–173
Retro Moderne (earrings), 126–129
Rings
    Bouquet, 130–133

Full Moon, 120–125
Rondelle beads, 140
    for Cascade necklace, 65
    for Deco Harvest pendant, 97
    for Spring Peas necklace, 70
    for Starburst bracelet, 27
    for Teardrop necklace, 41, 43
Round beads, 140
    for Deco Harvest pendant, 97
    for Starburst bracelet, 27
Round-nose pliers, 134
Ruby Drop (pendant), 74–77

Seed beads, 142
    for Bouquet, 131, 133
    Delica, 19, 152
    for Floating Pearls necklace, 37, 38
    for Infinity pendant, 85
    mixing, 151
    for Starburst bracelet, 27
Silk cord or thread, 143
Silver beads
    for Ruby Drop pendant, 75, 76
    for Trio necklace, 51, 52
Sizing tool, 123
Smart Beads, 109, 111
Spacer beads, 146
    for Bouquet, 131, 133
    for Water Lily pendant, 91, 92, 93, 95
Spring clamps, 135
Spring Peas (necklace), 70–73
Stackable vials, 137
Starburst (bracelet), 26–29
Starfish (pendant), 78–83
Sterling silver wire, 144
Stopper beads for Infinity pendant, 84, 86
Strand materials, 143
    connecting, 150–151
    crimping, 158–159
    stringing beads with, 148
Sunrise (necklace), 44–49

Teardrop beads, 141
    for Teardrop necklace, 41
Teardrop (necklace), 40–43
Thread-cutting scissors, 135
Tiger's eye tubes for Willow Branch necklace, 31, 35
Tools, basic, 134–139
Topaz beads for Classic Acorns pendant, 103
Transite, 143

for Ruby Drop pendant, 76
    for Venetian Swirl necklace, 61, 62, 63
    for Willow Branch necklace, 34, 35
Translucent beads, 142
    for Full Moon ring, 121
Trefoil (necklace), 54–59
Trio (necklace), 50–53
Tweezers, 136

Utility knife, 76
Venetian-style beads for Venetian Swirl necklace, 61, 62, 63
Venetian Swirl (necklace), 60–63

Water Lily (pendant), 90–95
Weaving Beads, 152–157
    for Liquid Gold bracelet, 20
Willow Branch (necklace), 30–35
    branch patterns for, 33
    making wrapped loop with stem for, 166–167
Wire, 144
    avoiding breaks in, 161
    cutting, 160
    manipulating thin, 161
    role of, in jewelry design, 161
    working with, 160
Wire brushes, 138
Wire cutters, 135
Wire loops, making a, 164–165
Wire wraps, 162–163
    making neat, 93
Wood block, 136
Wooden beads, 136
Wrapped loop with a stem, making, 166–167
Wrapped-wire loop
    making, 166–167
    for Pastel Cloud bracelet, 17
    for Sunrise necklace, 45, 46
    for Teardrop necklace, 42, 43

Zigzag (earrings), 112–115

...you like More Glamorous Beaded Jewelry
take a look at these other craft titles in our Home Arts series.

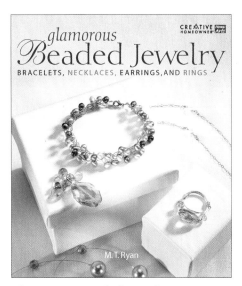

Glamorous Beaded Jewelry
ISBN: 978-1-58011-295-6
CH Book #265133
144 pages, 8$\frac{1}{2}$" x 9$\frac{1}{2}$"
$19.95 US / $24.95 CAN

The Color Book of Beaded Jewelry
ISBN: 978-1-58011-348-9
CH Book #265202
176 pages, 8$\frac{1}{2}$" x 9$\frac{1}{2}$"
$19.95 US / $24.95 CAN

Bead Style
ISBN: 978-1-58011-314-4
CH Book #265147
128 pages, 7$\frac{1}{4}$" x 10$\frac{7}{8}$"
$19.95 US / $24.95 CAN

The Decorated Bag
ISBN: 978-1-58011-296-3
CH Book #265138
144 pages, 8$\frac{1}{2}$" x 9$\frac{1}{2}$"
$19.95 US / $21.95 CAN